ISLAND IN THE CITY

A Post-war Childhood in a Community Defined by its Boundaries

Ray Noyes

WORDCATCHER publishing

ISLAND IN THE CITY
A Post-war Childhood in a Community Defined by its Boundaries
Wordcatcher History

© 2018 Ray Noyes

Cover design © David Norrington, for picture credits, see section after Contents.

The Author asserts the moral right to be identified as the author of this work. All rights reserved. This book is protected under the copyright laws of the United Kingdom. Any reproduction or other unauthorised use of the material or artwork herein is prohibited without the express written permission of the Publisher.

British Library Cataloguing in Publication Data.
A catalogue record for this book is available from the British Library.

No part of this book may be reproduced, stored in a retrieval system, or transmitted in any form or by any means, electronic, electrostatic, magnetic tape, mechanical, photocopying, recording or otherwise, without the written permission of the Publisher.

Published in the United Kingdom by Wordcatcher Publishing, Cardiff, UK.
www.wordcatcher.com.
Telephone: 02921 888321

Paperback format ISBN: 9781911265474

First Edition: 2019

Category: Social History / South Wales / Cardiff

CONTENTS

PICTURE CREDITS
PREFACE 1
CHAPTER ONE 3
   The Island
CHAPTER TWO 21
   The First Day
CHAPTER THREE 30
   D'you Want Coal or Ice Cream?
CHAPTER FOUR 35
   Boots and Clogs
CHAPTER FIVE 51
   Early Schooldays
CHAPTER SIX 76
   Going Places
CHAPTER SEVEN 90
   The Sound of Fire
CHAPTER EIGHT 107
   The Glory of Locomotion
CHAPTER NINE 115
   Horses and Carts
CHAPTER TEN 119
   Bombs
CHPTER ELEVEN 132
   Salt, Vinegar, Knives and Umbrellas
CHAPTER TWELVE 144
   Fancy Some Tripe?

CHAPTER THIRTEEN 153
  Oh, the Hokey-Kokey!

CHAPTER FOURTEEN 164
  Mrs S's Gloves

CHAPTER FIFTEEN 176
  Not Today, Thank You

CHAPTER SIXTEEN 183
  Money Singing on Wires

PICTURE CREDITS

Page	Image description	Acknowledgement
2	Map	Reproduced with the permission of National Library of Scotland
4	Shopping street	Reproduced with permission of Grangetown Local History Society
6	Grange Gardens	Reproduced with permission of Grangetown Local History Society
8	Speedway	Reproduced with permission from the Grangetown Local History Society
9	Kitchen	Reproduced with permission of Nick Hedges, nickhedgesphotography.co.uk
10	Shop	Ray Noyes
11	Lamp lighter	Reproduced with permission of Falkirk Community Archives
13	Dentist chair	Image copyright Alamy H7GK2E
15	Bogy	Kiz Crosbie. 2014, www.kizcrosbie.com
15	Ships in dock	Ray Noyes
16	Unloading	Ray Noyes
16	Dockside	Ray Noyes
16	Railway	Ben Brooksbank, (creative commons)
17	Dry docks	Ben Salter from 'Wales – Mount Stuart Dry Docks'
18	Fishing	Ray Noyes
21	Bike	Birmingham Museums Trust (creative commons)
24	Hopscotch	'Street Games' - Reproduced with permission from St Margaret's, London
26	Wagons	Reproduced with permission of Grangetown Local History Society
31	Coal cart	East Riding Archives
36	Furnaceman	National Archives
37	Steel works	© Alamy, EK2XD9
38	St Paul's	Ray Noyes
39	Chapel	Reproduced with permission of Grangetown Local History Society
40	Organ	Rolf Leibold
42	Coke oven	Creative commons Wikimedia.org
43	Gas works	Reproduced with permission of Grangetown Local History Society
44	Room	Rudi Winter, St Fagans
45	Pub	Reproduced with permission of Grangetown Local History Society
51	School	Reproduced with permission of Grangetown Local History Society
53	School	Ray Noyes
54	Marbles	Geoff Charles, 'Aspects of Amman Valley Life, 1949'
56	Classroom	© CSG CIC Glasgow Museums Collection
56	Pen etc	Ray Noyes
59	School	Ray Noyes
69	School	Ray Noyes
71	Book	Ray Noyes
75	School photo	Ray Noyes
76	Tram	Reproduced with permission of Grangetown Local History Society
77	Ticket	Medford Willow

78	Tram	Elliott Brown
79	Delivery bicycle	Obscurasky
79	Trolleybus	Reproduced with permission of Grangetown Local History Society
81	Bus	Craig Murphy
82	Bus	Les Chatfield
84	Bus	Oakeley Arms
86	Car and people	Ray Noyes
87	Car and people	Ray Noyes
88	Stove	B A Hiorth & Co
89	Ferry	Gordon Spicer
91	Docks	Lionel Walden
92	Statue	Ray Noyes
92	Exchange	Ray Noyes,
93	Building	Ray Noyes
96	Subway	Wales Online archives
97	Compartment	Simon Smiler
98	Train and bridge	Ashley Dace
99	Lorry	Reproduced with permission of Grangetown Local History Society
101	Car / motorbike	Car by Basher Eyre / Bike by 'p_a_h' image YUC605
103	Engine	Trevor Rickard
104	Train	Ben Brooksbank
105	Furnace	Alfred T Palmer
106	Painting	Lionel Walden
107	Station	Ray Noyes
107	Station hall	Ray Noyes
110	Exchange	Ray Noyes
113	Steamer	Reproduced with permission of Grangetown Local History Society
115	Horse and cart	Kind permission of Leeds Library and Information Services
116	Dray	Reproduced with permission of Grangetown Local History Society
118	Barrels of beer	From the Bundesarchiv
119	Bomb site	From Tyne and Wear Archives and Museums
120	Corner shop	Ray Noyes
122	Works	Reproduced with permission of Grangetown Local History Society
123	Stable	Ray Noyes
125	Gun	Jason Rogers, Hemel Hempstead
125	Caps	'Harry20'
127	Shed	Derek Harper
129	Shelter	Gareth Beynon
132	Washing	Roosevelt Presidential Library and Museum
135	Coronation	Biblioarchives, Canada
136	Car	'Charles01'
137	Car	Thomas' Pics
139	Knife Grinder	Reproduced with permission from Heritage Images, Picturemedia Ltd
140	Shop	Wolfgang Sauber
141	Car	Mike Peel (www.mikepeel.net)
141	Bus conductor	Ministry of Information, Photo Division. Imperial War Museum
144	Tripe	Charles Haynes

145	Advert	Ray Noyes
145	Pig's head	Jeremy Keith, Brighton and Hove
147	Ration book	Ray Noyes
147	ID card	Ray Noyes
148	Queue	Imperial War Museum
149	Arcade	Ray Noyes
150	Notice	Wellcomeimages.org
151	Bottles	With permission from Pat Cryer, webmaster of the 1900s Wartime Healthcare for Children website
155	Salvation Army	State Library of New South Wales
159	City hall	Stephen Elwyn Roddick
165	Portrait	Ray Noyes
166	Portrait	Ray Noyes
167	Howells	Ray Noyes
168	Shop	Jean-Pol Grandmont
171	Shop	Ray Noyes
175	Street party	Ray Noyes
176	Salesman	permission of Betterware Co Ltd
177	Soap	Wellcomeimages.org
178	Shelves of goods	Phil Sangwell from the Bygones Museum, Babcoombe
178	Tin	Petaholmes
179	Tin	The State Library of Queensland
179	Spray	Bullenwachter
186	Motor bike	Kim Traynor
188	Piano	Wikimedia Commons
193	Snow	Wales Online, History of Wales
194	Stove	With permission from Bradford on Avon Museum
197	Washing steps	With permission from Nick Hedges, nickhedgesphotography.co.uk

Cover images

Furnaceman	National Archives
Lamp lighter	Reproduced with permission of Falkirk Community Archives
Bombed house	Glamorgan Archives
Coal cart	East Riding Archives
Street party	Ray Noyes

PREFACE

I wrote the following reminiscences of my childhood for my grandchildren some years ago. They hadn't seen or experienced travelling in a steam train or known what it is to have a bath only once a week in front of a coal fire, while listening to the adventures of detective Dick Barton on the wireless. Re-reading them, I can re-enter my childhood and become the young, unformed and uncompromised person that I was then.

But now, after passing the biblical milestone of three score years and ten, these memories have an entirely richer meaning when placed within the context of the rest of my life, and especially what I believe I have now become. So, this is not so much a retrospective as an update on the child who features in the stories that I hope you'll enjoy reading.

My brother and I lived with our parents and grandparents in what is now something of a rare arrangement, but it was common then. As such, these stories are as much about them as me.

OS six-inch series, Scotland, 1892-1960, Grangetown, Cardiff

CHAPTER ONE
The Island

This may sound strange, but I was born and grew up on an island. It wasn't a tree-covered island, with shores lapped by the sea, but an urban one surrounded by its own seas of adventure and excitement: ones of roads, canals, docks and railways. Just like the sea, the areas surrounding our urban shores were mysterious and exciting, calling us, siren-like, to explore them. As with all island dwellers, we were curious as to what existed beyond it and this curiosity had to be satisfied, which resulted in a number of adventures.

On some of these near horizons lay lands which were very different to the island on which I lived. Some were industrial areas containing steel works, railway shunting yards, docks and gasworks. Others were slum areas dating from the mid 1800s. Yet others were tidal rivers, mud flats or railway tracks and the sea itself.

So, my island, although an urban one, was a special land to us, encircled by other districts of the city of Cardiff. It was an island of play; a land of adventure, strange sights, noises and smells: a land of pirates, cowboys, secret hideouts, danger and mock-heroes.

Unlike water-encircled islands, where inhabitants cannot easily leave, our barriers to travel were porous, so that the world around, once explored, seemed infinitely large. Although our parents warned us against travelling to those neighbouring areas, we often did, such adventures being the most thrilling of all.

Of course, when one is young (I'm talking about being between five and ten) the world does seem very large. Which is quite amusing, because when I look now at some of the industrial areas I shall be referring to, such as the docks, they seem quite modest. Perhaps all children's exaggerated sense of size is what makes the world around them so exciting.

The boundaries of our island were simple, but sometimes challenging. They comprised a busy major road to the north, which led to the city centre; the tidal River Taff to the east; a railway embankment to the west; and the docks to the south, the gateway to Tiger Bay. So my particular part of Cardiff, centred on my own street, felt as though it was surrounded on four sides by lands of a different character, each presenting excitement and occasionally danger.

My island was called Grangetown; a Victorian-built district of Cardiff, to the south-west of the city. It is a working class area, built with the intention of housing workers in the once burgeoning industrial areas nearby, such as Penarth Docks, an iron and steel works, the gasworks and railways. This time, in the 1850s, was one of huge growth for Cardiff and the surrounding area due to the Victorians' investment in the Industrial Revolution. In the early 20th century Cardiff was the largest coal-exporting docks in the world and its coal exchange set the price of the commodity world-wide.

Grangetown has an interesting history, having been at one time a grange of the monks of Margam Abbey. Taken over by lay investors after the Dissolution of the Monasteries, it eventually came into the hands of rich families such as the Windsor-Clives, the Earls of Plymouth and the Marquess of Bute. It is they who saw the area as suitable for housing the workers of their own industries, although the early inhabitants of the grange did not always enjoy living there; the houses had been built on a tidal marsh which caused not only health problems but also long-term construction problems.

Lessons learned from the early phases of the development resulted in much improved housing for the middle classes, together with comprehensive amenities, such as parks, schools, shops and places of worship, beside numerous public houses. With all these elements put into the mix, including different classes of people, the area grew up with multiple personalities and a rich cross-section of people and their activities. Add to this indigenous mix, the influx of foreign arrivals on

Paget Street shops

ships and railways and it is no surprise that Grangetown had and still has a very varied culture.

This very mixture has secured its survival. History tells us that island communities need fresh blood to survive or their culture can atrophy, and these arrivals came in marked numbers in the 1940s and 50s when I was young. It is this period of my life that I wish to share with you.

* * *

Although the streets and back lanes of Grangetown were, to our eyes, exciting places, if we wanted a change from playing games there, we also had green areas such as Grange Gardens, Sevenoaks Park or the Marl.

Grange Gardens was the posh, proper park, just two streets away from where I lived. Besides having a grumpy park-keeper or 'parky' who had a nice, brick-built hut to stay in (with a cosy coal fire in winter), the park had a permanent staff of two gardeners who tended the many flower beds and mowed the bowling green to billiard smoothness. They had a small green-painted shed tucked into shrubbery in a corner of the gardens which always seemed to be a very cosy arrangement. It seemed a pretty attractive job to me, because they had the liberty of the park in the sense of being able to walk on the grass if they wished and could, I assumed, do whatever work they decided needed doing. Added to this freedom, they could also hide out of sight in their little green hut, hidden amongst the bushes if they wished.

One of the salient features of the park was, and still is, the war memorial: a tall stone base, with bronze plaques containing the names of the many men and women who fell during the wars, surmounted by a statue of an angel holding an olive tree sapling. On summers' evenings, a brass band played near the memorial. Deck chairs would be set out and a very relaxing time could be had for older folk.

Men and women also played bowls and the green was always immaculately kept. Tennis was played by some, but not many, and it was generally unusual to see the courts used.

The geometric centre of the park, as now, was a large open circle, around the perimeter of which were numerous seats. In the summer, these would be occupied by people chatting and laughing. Children would play there in front of their parents and grandparents; ice creams would be imported from Dimascio's, the Italian ice cream shop just outside the park. The men, always in suits and waistcoats no matter the weather, would wander around looking at the roses and smoking, often with pipes. The women would talk to each other, many doing so whilst they knitted or did crochet. These activities were not merely hobbies, but were necessary. Socks, for example, wore out quickly, because they contained only pure wool, without the reinforcement of man-made fibres as they do now.

Grange Gardens

Socks were not elasticated, often falling in a roll around one's ankles. We boys, when wearing long socks, wore a wide elastic band beneath the turned-down top of a sock. Men, when wearing their best clothes, wore sock suspenders; a rather weird-looking band that fitted around the calf and dangled two straps that clipped onto the top of the sock to keep them up.

Jumpers they made too, as did my mother, although the knitting of socks in the park, being small items, was much easier than knitting a complete jumper!

On one side of the central circle a wooden shelter had been built, seemingly out of logs. It can be seen in the photograph above. Old folk, as well as youngsters often used this as a shelter when it rained. The parky always watched to see if anyone was using it for the wrong reasons, especially playing in there: parks were *not* for play!

Grange Gardens was a formal park, offering flower beds and herbaceous borders for everyone's appreciation, together with fine lawns and the shade from trees. I suppose you could call it a garden for grown-ups, and was very much appreciated, because every few people had gardens of their own. Almost all houses had small yards at their back, not gardens. It was therefore refreshing to see greenery and smell flowers. You can imagine, I think, that if you were someone who had been working in hot, dusty conditions, say, a stroll around or a sit down in such pleasant surroundings would be important to them.

For us children, the problem with this formal park was that the park-keeper would never allow us, or anyone else for that matter, to walk on the grass or to ride a bicycle there. We got over this latter difficulty by ensuring he was always patrolling on the opposite side of the park before launching ourselves and our bikes down one of the ramped entrances (Grange Gardens was lower than the surrounding streets in some parts). This usually gave us enough momentum to zoom right across the park and out the other side before he could chase us.

After emerging triumphant, we would pop across to Dimascio's for an ice cream, a gobstopper or other sweets. Their choice of liquorice was particularly good. They also sold something called Spanish Root. This looked like a twig and was the actual root of the liquorice plant. Once chewed and sucked (excellent for the teeth), it exuded a liquorice taste for hours. As one end became soggy and bedraggled, the other end was tackled. Those children with penknives would then cut off both straggly ends and have the small middle bit left, which they popped into their mouths whole. You shouldn't think that we children carried dangerous knives: most men and lots of children had a small penknife in their pockets with which to tackle all sorts of incidental tasks.

Dimascio's café was a favourite of ours and did a good trade from children leaving school in the afternoons. The school was just across the road from the shop.

Mr and Mrs Dimascio were one of many Italian couples who settled in Cardiff, both before the war and after it. It's sad to realise that some of those who had settled just before and during the war and who had not yet been granted resident status, were sometimes interned in prisoner of war camps. I do not think this happened to the Dimascio's. Britain was at war with Italy as well as with Germany during the Second World War, so people of such nationalities were, theoretically anyway, enemies of ours and could pass information to their birth country, via their continuing family contacts in those countries.

Dimascio's ice cream parlour was unusual, in that the counter and the walls were all lined with green glass, as were three small tables at which one could sit, giving it a most continental and rather cool look. Their ice cream was delicious!

There was a second park we played in where we were certainly allowed on the grass, for it was essentially a playing field. Sevenoaks Park on Ninian Road was large and given over to baseball. Matches were often staged during the early evening in summer and hundreds of families would gather to watch the matches and have picnics.

For our purposes, the park had, and still has, a feature which we always found useful, and that was the very high brick wall of the railway embankment. This offered excellent opportunities for chalking cricket stumps or football goals on it (no self-respecting child was without chalk in his or her pocket). It also had the best formal play equipment of the nearby parks available to us.

Speedway programme from 1951

As for the Marl, which is a very large playing field to the south of Grangetown, we didn't use it much because it had a harsh surface beneath any grass that grew on it. Marl is a lime-rich clay, containing grit. Before it was grassed over, it served as a speedway circuit for our bikes. In the summer it was full of dust, as our bikes tore around our makeshift circuit, racing each other and emulating the professional speedway riders who raced on the big circuit on Penarth Road, to which my father and I used to go. It was also good for football, but the grit gave a nasty graze if a player fell on it.

The Marl was deep in lower Grangetown territory; this was an area containing the oldest and smallest terraced houses, built in the 19th century. The streets adjacent to the Marl were notorious for minor crime; it was not an area to venture into alone, especially on a bike, because the rider could return bike-less. One had to be on the lookout for gangs of tough lads who might decide to give you a beating whilst taking just about anything they found on you; although venture I did, many times and at some speed, reckoning that a commando-like strike would be wiser than meandering around inviting guerrilla attacks from rough lads. Lower Grangetown even had its own dedicated police station and its own prison cells.

Our street, Penhevad Street, was pretty well the limit of the nicer part of Grangetown. This may sound snobbish, but that's just how it was. The houses were built much later than those in lower Grangetown; they were larger and built to a higher standard. The street ran east-west, parallel to the nicest street of all, Pentrebane

Typical 1950s kitchen

Street, which not only overlooked Grange Gardens but also boasted a Roman Catholic Church and its priest's house; no other street contained such prestigious establishments.

Many, if not most, of my primary and junior school pals lived in lower Grangetown, so I knew very well from visiting them how different their houses were to ours. Sorry to say, one of the strongest and lasting memories of those differences was the smell. The houses were very small and terraced, sometimes 'two up, two down', and had no bathrooms. Their front doors opened directly onto the street and their back yards were often of beaten earth or concrete.

Most houses had just one inside tap, in the kitchen. All washing was done there, of clothes as well as bodies, and of course cooking. Privacy was at a minimum in such houses. Usually the tap was fixed above a deep porcelain Bosch or sink. Hot water was not always available and had to be heated on the fire in the living room.

My best friend in junior school, Richard, lived in one such house, in Knole Street. At one end of the street, one of Grangetown's most heavily used amenities was situated, the so-called Iron Room. It had been a gift of the Baroness Windsor in 1861, the constructor of Grangetown, and was supposed to double up as a school and a church. It belonged to the C of E church, St Paul's, which was close by. On Tuesdays, in the summer months, a film (often a silent one) would sometimes be shown; I suppose with the aim of making us behave ourselves.

Directly across the road from the Iron Room was, and still is, one of Cardiff's most famous food shops, Clark's Pie Shop. Here the 'world-famous' pies were originally made.

Richard and I used to often get together to play soccer with friends and a few times he'd stay overnight at my house, playing games and having pillow fights. My first sleepover with him in his house, however, remains a vivid memory to this day.

I'd knocked on his door before to call for him, so I knew his house, but hadn't actually been inside it. The passageway was very dark, the walls being painted dark brown up as far as the dado line.

I remember being surprised by the flaking paint (as well as the dark colours) because his father, Jack, used to work in a paint works (the Navigation Paint Company Ltd), adjacent to the gasworks. I assumed that if anyone were to have nice bright colours everywhere in his house, it would be the son of a paint works worker.

The house was damp, being built originally on a marsh (as much of Grangetown was). The kitchen and living room were one, so that cooking smells and leaking gas all contributed to a smelly cocktail which was pervasive.

Clarke's Pie Shop

Most of the cooking was done on an open fire in the living room. A large cast iron 'range', as they were called, contained an oven and various trivets, on which saucepans could be placed and which swung over the fire. Such ranges were ubiquitous in this part of Grangetown and provided all the cooking facilities. Of course, cooking smells remained in the room. The coal fire was essential for cooking food but also for heating water. Even in summer the fire was kept going so as to be able to cook and to heat water, which was not always comfortable in warm weather.

The middle or living room/kitchen had just one window, which overlooked the yard, but was so dirty it was of little help in lighting the room. This middle room (sandwiched between the front room and scullery) had no carpeting, just lino on the floor. A sideboard, with the most enormous bulbous turned legs plus two armchairs completed the inventory of furniture.

Throughout the first evening meal I wasn't hungry; the smell kept interfering with my appetite. Going up to bed, his mother, Phyllis (a very large person - in terms of height as well as musculature), preceded us, whilst his father, a diminutive man with spikey hair, lit the gas light hanging from the hall ceiling.

To digress for a moment, I was familiar with gas lighting because our house had it too, but by this time we also had electricity so that we rarely used our gaslights. I always enjoyed watching the procedure for lighting gas fittings. They could be a source of some amusement and even danger. Firstly, gas fittings hanging from ceilings or attached to walls looked rather strange. They had chains dangling from them with small rings on the end, by which the fittings would be switched on or off by pulling on one of them.

The chains were attached to either end of a short bar, which, as it tilted, operated the gas valve. The angle taken up by this bar determined how much gas, and therefore light, could be obtained. For high ceilings, the operating chains could be very long. A hook on a long pole, enabling one chain or the other to be pulled, then engaged the rings on the chains. In our chapel and Sunday School, these chains were very long indeed, the lights being very high up.

I always found the delicate silk mantels surrounding the gas fittings within the flame to be rather amazing. They were extremely fragile, made of the finest cotton. I always wondered how such a delicate thing could emit light. The solution was a very clever one. When a new mantel was first lit, it would literally burn to ash, the cotton catching fire and leaving behind a very delicate residue of an exotic metal such as Thorium. It was this metal that when heated by the flame, glowed incandescent with a brilliant white light that illuminated the room. (Later in life I learned that Thorium is radioactive!)

Gas lighter, Jackson Avenue, Falkirk – typical of those found in Grangetown

The second fascinating aspect of gaslights was the ignition process. Most people kept long wax spills in a pot on the mantelpiece, which they lit from the fire. If they couldn't afford spills they used rolled-up newspaper, which could be quite dangerous and messy. If the person lighting the gas co-ordinated the offering of the lighted spill with the release of gas, it lit with a gentle 'poof' sound. The silk mantle of the light, previously burned to a fine and extremely delicate white ash, would then begin to glow, whiter and whiter, until the light could be quite bright. But many gas fittings were burned at a lower level to save on gas which barely improved on candle light; in the summer, the heat gas lights produced was not welcome.

If, however, the flaming spill was offered to the already hissing gas, there could be enough gas and air to blow out the taper's flame. Then, unlit gas continued to hiss out until either the 'off' chain was pulled, or, more excitingly, a freshly lit spill was offered up and the gas exploded. The gas then collected in a cloud around the ceiling, and this cloud would light with a dull thump and an attractive blue flame, scorching the ceiling (or the wall if it was a wall fitting). All gas lights had scorch marks around them.

All street lights were also lit by gas. In the evenings, a lamplighter would cycle around the streets with a short wooden ladder over one shoulder which he placed up against the horizontal cross arms of lamp standards.

Mounting the ladder, he would open the glass door of the lamp, wipe both sides of the glass panes and then wind up and set the clockwork time clock inside. It would be set for however many hours he thought the light ought to shine and it would switch off the gas in the morning.

He would light the lamp with a special long, flint lighter. Once he was happy with the brightness of the light, which took a little while to develop as it heated up, off he'd go to the next lamp.

This took so much time for an area like ours, which had many streets, that some lamps were lit well before sundown, whilst others lit up when it was almost dark. He therefore varied his rounds so that the same lamps were not always lit at the same time.

It's interesting to note that the lamplighter had to be proficient not only in maintaining clockwork mechanisms but also at cleaning and adjusting gas valves and, of course, being able to ride a bike with a ladder on his shoulder. I don't know if the gas company (it was not nationalised until 1947) provided his bicycle or not. They certainly did not provide his suit.

He was a middle-aged man who only ever seemed to wear the one brown suit, a habit common amongst working men. It was rare that employers provided work clothing. Suits and even trilby hats were worn all day and every day, from attending the day job to gardening. My grandfather, for example, wore his trilby and waistcoat even when digging his allotment. Men would dress like this even when sitting on a sandy beach. There was simply no other form of clothing. Leisure clothing for men came into fashion in the 50s. And even then long sleeves predominated and colours were sombre.

Our lamplighter had something wrong with his neck and could barely turn it, so he wasn't always able to avoid traffic or other obstacles as well as he ought.

***

To return to Richard's dark house, we weren't given the option of having a wash or cleaning our teeth before going to bed. It just wasn't done. The ensuing dental cavities was probably why nearly every adult at that time had false teeth. It was very common for adults to have all their teeth removed, sometimes in one go, and to have false ones fitted, the argument being that if that were not done, they'd only have to suffer toothache anyway, so they may as well get rid of their teeth before decay really set in.

False teeth were not always a good fit. They were often loose and became a source of amusement; they sometimes fell out when someone laughed or ate something sticky. In fact, many a person removed his or her teeth at the table before beginning a meal so as to avoid having to remove them in the middle of eating.

Those wishing to avoid embarrassment when undertaking this manoeuvre would do so secretively and wrap them in either a handkerchief or a table napkin. But one of my aunts seemed to delight in simply placing them on the table in front of her and, of course, in front of us. It was not a sight to engender a healthy appetite.

I only went to the dentist when in pain and it usually meant an extraction under gas, which was an awful experience, until local anaesthetics started to be used.

Dentist's chair

A hard rubber block was placed in the mouth to keep it open and then a rubber mask (the smell of which I can still remember) was placed over the face and nitrous oxide gas was breathed in causing unconsciousness. When waking up, many patients were sick and unable to stand, so you had to have a good friend or parent with you to take you home. If the gas hadn't properly knocked out the patient, then he simply suffered. If too much had been inhaled, he was sick and often wouldn't come round for some time. A visit to the dentist was to be feared for the sheer barbarity of it.

We should also remember the crude equipment available at that time. The delicate high-speed air-driven drills we have now had not been invented. Instead, a pedal-driven slow-speed drill was used. The dentist would stand on one leg and push on a plate that, due to gearing, would rotate a long rubber band that ran up to the top of the device and down onto the drill. The drill rotated slowly and painfully and was used without anaesthetic, unless you were having an extraction. So the patient was either gassed into total unconsciousness for an extraction or told not to make a fuss and suffer a filling. No wonder many an adult had all their teeth out in one go rather than suffer repeated torture, one at a time.

Richard's bedroom was in the back of the house. He shared it with his brother, Martin. A china pot under his bed was our joint toilet for the night. Besides the mild embarrassment, having an open pot of urine under the bed gave all bedrooms the same easily identified odour. Their use by women was not easy or comfortable and many a bedroom mat was damp by the morning. It was nice to return home the next day to carpeted floors and an outside loo. What luxury!

* * *

Our sources of amusement and the games we played were not dependent upon having green spaces; much of our time was spent either on our bikes or in the lanes constructing things, such as 'bogies'. These were crude vehicles built from a simple plank of wood on which to sit, and a pair of wheels front and back, usually pram wheels. The front pair was used to steer, usually by pulling on string attached to each end.

We used to have races with these, although it was really in the construction of them that the interest lay. Saws, hammers and nails, lots of them, were required, as well as some idea as to how to make the front pair of wheels turn smoothly without jamming on the plank, which was always the weak point of the design. Once made, the driver had to be pushed from behind, or find a hill somewhere. The best one was at the back of my Aunty Flo's. Here, a steep hill descends into the lane and opens out not far from the bottom, thus allowing space in which to turn around.

Bogy cart

Ships in dock

They were really great things to play on, but it was not easy to maintain one's seat if moving at speed around a corner. The narrow plank rarely had anything as sophisticated as a seat and so the driver often fell off and was sometimes run over by the thing. Having someone to push you on level ground was a lot safer, although it was hard work for them.

Failing any group activity, it seemed as though we lived all day on our bikes. It was our default option if we didn't know what to do and in spite of excellent public transport, we cycled long distances: to Barry, Porthkerry, Swanbridge, Castell Coch and all places in between. To cover 20 to 30 miles in a day was not unusual. Bearing in mind that bikes were very heavy, with chain guards, steel mudguards and just three gears (if we were lucky) and to this we added loaded saddle bags containing our food and other items for the day: 30 miles wasn't bad going for young children.

Bikes were particularly good for exploring and our preferred adventure zone was the docks. Although there were manned dock gates at Bute Street, we were never stopped from entering the area. At these gates, numerous men would queue up looking for work as stevedores, especially if word got around that a new ship had just docked and needed unloading, by hand of course.

It took days to unload a cargo ship. Items were lifted individually from the hold of the ship, piled into a large rope net attached to the crane, and then placed onto the quayside where they had to be again man-handled onto transport, often the railway, or stacked in adjacent warehouses.

Moving goods was very labour-intensive and tiring work. Ship owners wanted their ships unloaded as quickly as possible, so foremen were pretty brutal in their search for speed, employing only the fittest men.

In spite of the fascination that ships afforded, our attention was always caught by the way that coal was loaded into ships – never *out* of them, of course, Cardiff being the world's largest coal-exporting port. It was the Great West Dock, the Roath Dock and the Queen's Dock (named after Queen Alexandra) where coal ships were loaded and where numerous semi-automatic wagon tippers were at work, fed with wagons from huge sidings.

These coal tippers were crane-like devices, one of which is preserved there still, where complete wagons of coal would be tipped into the ships' holds. They were fixed on the very edge of the dock, overlooking the ship's hold.

As a wagon came into the rear of them, they lifted up the entire wagon of coal, emptying it into the hold in one go. When all the loose coal had left the wagon, a clever automatic device would scrape clean the bottom of it. Nothing was wasted. In spite of water being sprayed onto the coal, the procedure created enormous clouds of coal dust. The quay was literally inches deep in it. The men who operated these dockside cranes were completely covered in it and must have suffered awful chest complaints. We were able to station ourselves and our bikes so as to be able to watch these unloading operations.

We would also not only monitor steam train movements but also ride alongside them, following them wherever they went across the docks, which may be considered

Top: Unloading ship by hand
Middle: Coal-tipping crane
Bottom: Railway sidings, Splott

pretty dangerous to modern eyes. After unloading their coal, they would eventually end up in large marshalling yards where trains of empty wagons were arranged ready to return to various collieries and steel works.

Our mothers always knew when we'd been watching coal-tipping operations because we'd return home covered in coal dust. They thought our activities dangerous, which I suppose they were. Cycling alongside a rolling steam engine could be quite tricky, especially if a bicycle wheel became trapped in a sunken railway line.

Watching ships come and go was an obvious thing to do at the docks, admiring the skill of the pilots and captains as they manoeuvred ships into tight berths. But not all of them were afloat; some were in dry dock being repaired. Three of these docks are still there, behind what is now Techniquest, which occupies the very site of the workshops serving the docks. In fact, the shape of the current building mimics closely the shape of the workshops.

Although it was rare that we were allowed down into the dry dock itself, by peering over the edge we realised just how much of a ship is under water, something we didn't realise seeing them afloat. The father of one of my closest friends was the manager at these

Mount Stuart Dry Docks

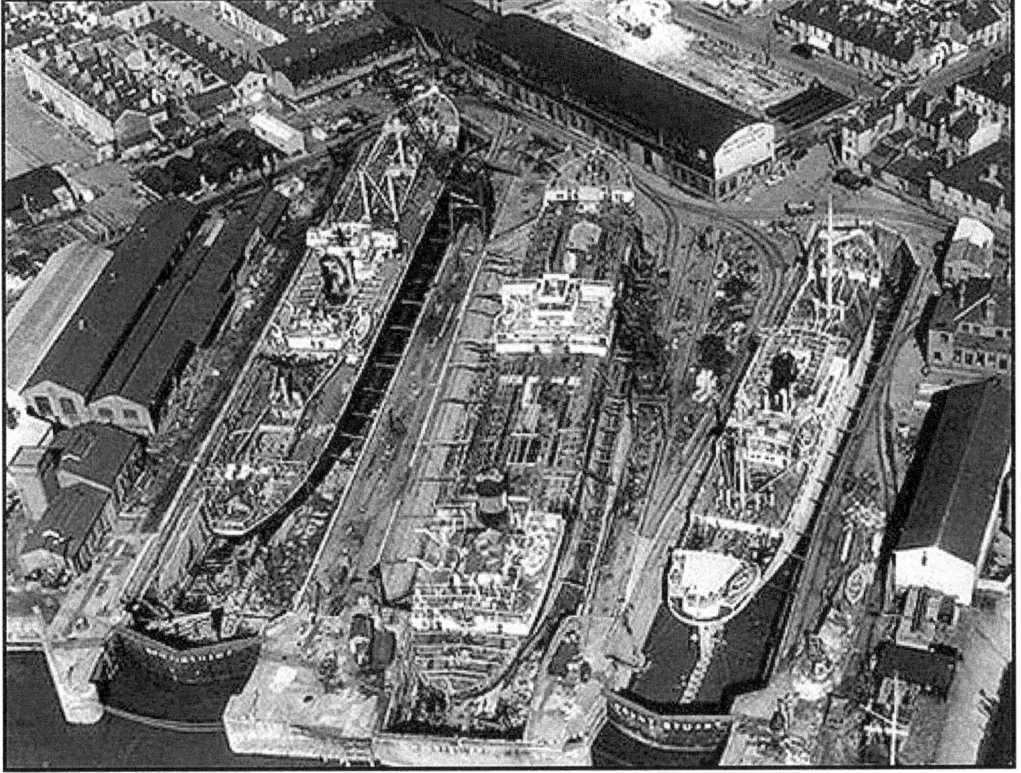

docks and repair facilities, so he occasionally took us around to watch the large-scale engineering work.

The docks dealt not only in coal, of course, but also in timber, much of it for pit props for the mines. Most came from Norway, which accounts for Cardiff's close relationship with that country. Roald Dahl's father (a Norwegian immigrant) set up a timber business dealing in just this trade. The establishment of the Norwegian Church is an enduring legacy of those close ties, although it was not always in its current position, but well within the docks themselves.

The logs would arrive in long lengths and needed cutting to size and trimming. This was done in the saw mills which were situated mainly to the west of the dock area, near the Taff. Finished props were stored in tall stacks on the canal side or adjacent to railway sidings for transport to the mines, but before they were cut they would be stacked in the most enormous piles before being thrown into large ponds.

This may sound odd but was a smart technique for softening the wood prior to cutting. The technique also made the stripping of bark much easier and helped to wash out impurities that could blunt the large-diameter saws that were powered by steam engines.

There were two such ponds called timber floats (Americans call them log ponds); one fed by the Taff and the other by water from the canal. They were dangerous facilities: if one tried to walk on floating logs and slipped into the water the logs would close over the victim and prevent him from surfacing. But as the timber trade declined and the 'floats', as we called them, gradually emptied, they offered good fishing, something I enjoyed, whilst all the time

Fishing on The Float timber pond

looking rather fearfully at the partially log-covered surface and wondering what grizzly sight may lie beneath.

Some of the more exotic home ports of ships tested our imaginations and our geography. Ships bringing timber from South America and Africa were especially interesting – at least their crew were. The sailors from these countries would bring their music with them and look for places to play.

The Packet on Bute Street was one pub which hosted such musicians, but there was a better one, the Navigator I think it was called, although I may be wrong, which stood on the corner of James Street and Adelaide Street. Here, many musicians from all over the world would gather ad hoc, to play jazz of an evening, a medium that by-passes all language.

The pub had twin swing doors right on the corner of it and two steps leading up to it. I used to sit there occasionally and listen. An old upright piano was just inside the door on the right and in effect if the doors were open in the summer, which they were, the players were just a few feet away from me.

One particular man played a really broken down, badly-marked old guitar and was a regular there. Dad knew him, but I can't remember his name. Could he get a tune out of that old thing! He was old when I first saw him and his deeply creased face (he was West Indian) was like tanned leather. He wore the thickest glasses I've seen; so thick it was impossible to see his eyes. Often wearing a woollen hat, even in summer, and a brown tweed jacket, he was a quiet, gentle man who came alive when his old, scratched guitar was in his hands.

I don't know if he worked, or was old enough to have retired – the latter probably – but he never drank alcohol, always opting for ginger beer and he gave me one once, which is how I know. He smoked cigarettes that had dark brown paper around them and which had a very odd smell. He pierced his lighted cigarette onto a guitar string at the neck of the instrument when he played, which made it jump up and down and often wasted away. I don't think he actually smoked very many, because there always seemed to be a cigarette burning at the neck of his guitar.

His speciality was what I would call 'swing blues': nothing fast, nothing fancy, but he had a style that was strong and rhythmic. He would occasionally sing, but always resisted for a long time before giving in. He seemed shy and since he was playing almost in the doorway, looking at the piano, he effectively had his back to the pub and was playing for the world outside. For me, in effect.

Various wind players also turned up, as well as more guitarists – always plenty of them – mandolin players, accordionists and trumpeters. East European sailors would bring strange instruments with them, not all of which would complement what was already being played, but it didn't seem to matter. They were particularly keen on singing their national songs and some had pretty fine voices, usually baritone. What a pub! What a golden opportunity to soak up live music and it was free.

I had begun taking piano lessons when almost six years old. I remember distinctly the very moment when I decided I wanted to play the instrument. It was a Saturday morning and I was listening to a jazz programme on the wireless and heard a violin and piano combination; it could have been Stephane Grappelli and George Shearing.

I remember going straight away into the front room where Dad was playing the piano and asked him then and there if I could learn to play like him. I often sat on a chair which was directly alongside the piano and watched his fingers. In particular I was struck by the obvious emotional satisfaction it gave him. It wasn't only that sound I wanted to create, but also to savour some of that pleasure. He was delighted with my enthusiasm and fixed me up with a Mr F to have lessons.

Mr F lived with his wife and spinster sister (the latter teaching violin) in the next street. He was very old and very slow (and had a small blue spot on his lower lip that always drew my attention), but was flexible about his teaching methods, in as much as he didn't mind me learning popular music as well as the classics. I decided early on that I didn't want to study for examinations but wanted to just get on with it and play music and he went along with that, my father included. So began for me a lifetime of pleasure playing the piano.

What a rich field of interest my urban island offered a child growing up. It wasn't very grand and had some seedy sides to it, but these too provided an education of sorts. I'm so glad I didn't grow up in a perfectly manicured cul-de-sac in a middle class district, which is precisely what I condemned my children to, I'm afraid.

CHAPTER TWO
The First Day

It was the first day of the school summer holidays, a day that was always bright, sunny and full of potential. Six weeks of such days stretched ahead. They were in the bank as it were; a deposit account of fun ready to be spent as we wished.

School summer holidays were always like this. Getting up earlier than usual, running excitedly out to the back lane where no one had appeared yet, its pregnant emptiness speaking of weeks of adventure to come. The sun encouraged the smells of brick, stone and tarmac to lift into the air. The lane was a stage on which six weeks of fun could be performed, and our fun recorded, literally, in the form of hopscotches.

This was a time when equipment was neither available nor necessary in order to entertain us. We found fun and pleasure in our inventiveness; our imagination creating games out of the simplest things: a football or a bicycle being the exceptions to this rule.

These were expensive items and were looked after very carefully. Having a bicycle, whether new or old, was something we all aspired to and many were offered by parents as rewards for examinations passed or by grandparents for a special birthday. This is the sort of bike I had as a reward for passing the eleven-plus exam to get in to grammar school. Such bikes were built for comfort and carrying things, not for speed. Wide, leather saddles and an upright position made for a relaxing ride, but they were very heavy.

BSA bicycle

There were very few what we called 'racing bikes' around. They were for the rather odd people who saw cycling as a sport, whereas the rest of us regarded it as a necessary means of transporting both ourselves and our shopping; ours were workhorses. Additionally, the idea of having very thin, fragile wheels and tyres on racing bikes didn't seem sensible when riding over rough roads. Having to bend double, reducing one's view of the road ahead, also seemed very odd.

In some ways, having a second-hand bike was more precious than having a new one, because it gave us the challenge of rebuilding it, thus learning mechanical skills and of course feeling a close attachment with our achievement. Hunting for spare parts was all part of the challenge. Repairing derailleur gears or even fully enclosed Sturmey Archer ones, was quite a challenge and learning when a part was worn beyond repair was as important as knowing when something was still repairable: these were important skills when eventually owning a car, for example.

Footballs, on the other hand, especially leather ones, were regarded as something particularly special and were nearly always obtained new. The leather, as with our football boots, was always looked after by being routinely treated to a coating of dubbin. The bladder inside was of fragile rubber and therefore was often punctured, but we became skilled at repairing that too, using a bicycle puncture repair kit.

So as we interacted with, and cared for, our equipment, we became practiced at looking after it and acquiring modest maintenance skills. The idea of throwing items away because they had a minor fault was not only anathema but something that never entered our minds. All we owned and all that surrounded us was valued, was repaired and was generally repairable.

This lesson applied to clothes, which were stitched and repaired, and to shoes which were resoled. Most families had a shoemaker's last in the garden shed. Handy packs of rubber soles and heels with tacks were available everywhere and could be cut to size.

New shoes were bought only as our feet outgrew our current ones or our old shoes had been so frequently resoled, that the leather base was peppered with holes from numerous previous tacks. All shoes were of leather, of course and just like our footballs, required regular waxing to maintain them.

Most shoes and especially ankle-length boots, which most young children and men wore, were given extra life immediately they left the shop, by nailing steel tips to them and hobnails. The latter were peppered on the soles in the form of dome-headed nails, whilst the former were curved plates nailed to the heels. Having a pair of freshly nailed boots was a privilege, not only for their newness, but also because of the special noise they made as we walked and the sparks we could strike from them on stone pavements

This, then, was the basic level of enjoyment we extracted from the world around us and it meant that we used the simplest, everyday things with which to make our lives interesting.

It can be imagined that when the summer holidays came, we could extend the appreciation of the simple by inventing and creating completely new things to do and to interest us. Except for our bicycles and footballs, we used whatever we could find around us to create something that challenged and enthused us. The simplest of these was a lump of chalk, with which to draw a hopscotch and to use in other games.

Some hopscotches were square, Sudoku-like mazes, full of numbers; others were linear from 1 to 10 with pairs of squares after 3 and 6. All were the focus of competition, often between girls and boys. Girls often did well at hopscotch because they were more measured in their approach. Boys, on the other hand, tried perhaps too hard to out-do everyone else by being overly competitive.

Square hopscotches were the most difficult because they didn't permit two feet to touch the ground at any time and were usually played by older children. They could be quite large, because there was no limit to the number of squares that could be drawn. The linear ones allowed a rest on two feet at squares 4/5 and 7/8, at least.

Ten squares seemed to be the standard size; but in both versions, part of the secret of success was how well we could throw our individual stone onto a specific square and get it to stay there without rolling out of the puzzle or onto the wrong square. The trick, of course, was to find a stone that was flat; the very best kind being a piece of slate. There were no rules as to the form of our personal stones and once we had found one that worked well for us, we treasured it, keeping it throughout the hopscotch season.

Drawing a hopscotch on the tarmac was the opening ceremony of the season, although not all lanes were surfaced with tarmac. Such lanes that were, were especially favoured for this. Experience

Children playing hopscotch

in drawing them counted for a lot and it was the older children who usually undertook the job of drawing the hopscotch. They knew the designs, the formula of generations of children past.

We thought of them as being the keepers of these ancient runes and the drawing of them was almost ceremonial, especially the very first one. Where would it be drawn? Who should do it? How large should it be?

Although they would become fainter as the season progressed, due to our feet gradually rubbing them out or by a (very rare, it seemed) shower of rain, it was a simple matter to go over a hopscotch with fresh chalk and reinvigorate it.

Groups would gather in the lane as word spread that so-and-so was going to draw a hopscotch. Immediately, rivalry would begin, as some children were chosen to play on a particular team whilst others were pushed out to join another group somewhere else. To be known and befriended by the senior architect earned one a certain cachet; but whichever team one eventually joined, these chalk drawings ensured a summer of competition and fun throughout the area, for there were many drawn in different lanes and competitions opened up between them.

These drawings were not to be altered and must last for the whole summer, so their lines had to be correct at the first attempt. They were often drawn with the aid of pieces of wood for a straight edge, usually taken from the tool shed of some unsuspecting father. But it was the chalk itself that presented the greatest challenge when setting out a hopscotch, because we didn't possess expensive sticks of school chalk. A substitute had first to be found.

Big lumps, as large as a fist, were sometimes used. To possess such a lump already marked one out as an expert in the game. It was regarded as a talisman, bringing good luck in the forthcoming competitions and showed that the possessor was a professional and meant business. Anyone turning up with a stick of chalk that had been purchased by someone's overly-protective mother was seen as rather sissy.

The largest lumps of chalk were obtained from a lime stack at the gasworks. It was essential to pick one with especial care: firstly because the hot lime stack was very dangerous in itself and secondly it contained many lumps which were not suitable. Pick up a lump of lime that had not been fully slaked by the rain with your bare hands and the burn would pass through your skin very painfully, which was a danger that added to the status of those who had such chalk talismans.

The particular stack of lime we raided was piled up in the shape of a volcano in the gasworks and the heat from it could be felt some distance away, especially after it rained. The heat seemed to give it a latent power and perhaps imparted a special quality to our lime chalk and to the bravery needed to obtain one. This was not a task for the girls, although they rarely went without one, because boys usually gave them as presents to those they wished to befriend.

We would approach the lime stack only on a dry day, for the least humidity would generate great heat in the volcano-like mound. Luckily, those lumps which had already reacted with water, were heavier than pure lime, and clumped together.

Being heavy, they would roll down the volcano and come to rest near its base, making them easy to identify and safe to pick up. As if escaping the dangerous volcano weren't daring enough, we also had to escape the site watchman, whose job it was to ensure we didn't succeed.

Once at the gasworks gate (shown in the background of the photograph below) we chose our lump from afar and discussed who should have which one. Each of us would then dash up to the steaming altar and grab the lump we had decided would be ours. But first of all, we had to make sure the watchman either wasn't there, or was fully occupied. It was usually a matter of patience. Waiting for the busy man to be called away to the weighbridge to weigh some railway wagons carrying tar or coal, we seized our chance. Lorries too helped us; they always stopped at the weighbridge and exchanged paperwork or asked for directions. Nipping around the blind side of one and walking with it into the works ensured the watchman didn't see us.

The watchman lived in a small brick hut built to the right of the gates. He guarded not only this steaming heap of lime but also piles of coal, heaps of sand and similar materials in use by the gasworks. Besides operating the weighbridge, he was responsible for opening the gates for trains to enter and leave the works. So he could be very busy. It was when a long train used the weighbridge that we had our very best chance of approaching the hot lime stack. This occasionally meant a long wait, but it was worth it.

Sneaking behind the rolling wagons, the stack was not more than a hundred yards off to the right, near the high wall of the railway embankment and we usually had enough time to get our chalk and beat it before he heard or saw us.

Playmates whose mothers heard of our daring exploits at the gasworks insisted on buying their loved ones commercial sticks of chalk. These well-meaning mums didn't realise the shame such a purchase brought down on their children. This may sound an overly simplistic, almost silly attitude,

The gasworks entrance in the distance and a line of tar wagons leaving the works

but we kids developed and shared a gang ethos. One shouldn't be able to buy oneself out of doing risky things, or buy oneself any kind of advancement whilst others had to either work hard for what they got, or had to take risks. Things that were bought were worth less than things that were made; or in our case, stolen. The children of parents who were relatively well off were considered cheats, because they didn't understand our ethos of striving for what we had.

Those with sticks of what we called school chalk, were therefore not often members of our hopscotch fraternity, being far too tied to their mothers' apron strings to come roaming the lanes looking for a challenge. Their mothers were those who wanted them not to wander far, nor to disappear from within hailing distance into foreign territories, getting up to who knows what mischief. They may even wash their hands before meals and carry a handkerchief.

Such excessive concern was a pity, because their mothers' very protectiveness denied their children learning how to avoid danger from the burning lime stack and the wrath of the watchman at the gasworks, besides generally allowing free rein to their naturally adventurous natures. I suppose we as a society are now overly protective in a similar way and may have developed a generic aversion to risk and adventure and their management.

But this is still the first day. Hopscotch in the lanes served not only as an introduction to the holidays, but also as an invitation to form groups or gangs, which perhaps sounds rather ominous these days. Our gangs formed innocently around a hopscotch, allowing individuals to show their stamina and accuracy in the game.

Naturally, each team leader wanted the best players, but we all realised that good players must also be likeable players. We quickly discovered not only who played well, but also who could be trusted to share in the secrets of our other games and activities. Enid Blyton's Secret Seven was emulated right across Grangetown, setting up adventures and competitions of all sorts. He or she who hatched up new ideas, the more bizarre and adventurous the better, was our natural leader.

Of course there were other games to play, such as individual and group skipping, which the girls were particularly fond of. For the latter version, they would find a long length of rope and try and see how many girls could skip within it. Three of four was not unusual. For some reason, we boys didn't go in for it as much. We also used spinning tops, wooden ones, that would be whipped to keep them going. Hoola hoops became popular as was the simplest and possibly the oldest toy: the yo-yo, learning the latest technique, such as 'walking the dog', 'the cast' or 'the spinner' (throwing it down firmly and allowing the yo-yo to spin freely before being brought back up).

Cowboys fought Indians, cops fought robbers, and games of 'touch' gave us lots of exercise as we ran furiously to eliminate one opponent after another by touching them. Rugby, using a stuffed sock, and cricket were also popular, but we reserved soccer for playing on grass, so as not to damage the leather soccer balls.

The problem with all ball games was the risk of losing the ball over someone's back wall (or smashing a window); sometimes the ball was never to be seen again. But most neighbours were good enough to throw them back or allow us into their yards to retrieve them; but for those who didn't, and we kept a mental note of them, we had to occasionally mount an SAS raid on their yard by climbing over the wall when they were out. Who would dare to do it? Would there be a dog in there who would corner our hero? Would he ever be seen again?

A form of polo, played on our bikes, was fun, if rather dangerous, because of the clashing of steel bicycle frames and the entangling of pedals and handle bars. Grazes due to falls were frequent too. But no self-respecting boy would get through the summer holidays without skin missing and wounds to boast about.

Another popular group game was hide and seek. Two groups would form up and after the toss of a coin, one would set off to hide, after the searching team had counted to a hundred (which we managed to do amazingly quickly!), each member having a lump of chalk. The chalk would be used to put an arrow on a wall or pavement showing which way the evading team had supposedly gone. The trick, of course, was for the evading team to draw the arrow in the wrong direction, sending one of the gang the wrong way to make further false marks and eventually return to the main gang at a prearranged spot.

The game tested our stamina; we would run through many streets and back lanes, the whole of the island being our patch. Hunts often took place in the older parts, those that were built in the mid-19th century and which were, de facto, the roughest quarter. It was simply more exciting there, where we encountered all manner of people, some strange and some a little frightening. The lanes and streets were also more numerous, narrow and sometimes had odd twists and turns in them.

There was no rear access lane between the back yards of the older houses, having been built back-to-back. The back of each house was therefore only yards from its rear neighbour. This high density and the tiny size of the houses (frequently of two bedrooms upstairs and two rooms downstairs) added to the impression of poverty. This may sound a harsh judgement, but poverty was a reality in those days.

These older streets were built in the 1850s and 1860s to house workers at the new gasworks, the Grangetown brick works, Penarth Docks, the tar works and a foundry.

CHAPTER THREE
D'you Want Coal or Ice Cream?

Mrs B kept the dairy, dispensing milk from churns into whatever jug or pot we brought along. Mr B, however, was out all day and had two faces: during the cold months of the year, his horse and heavy wagon would deliver coal in tough, open hessian sacks which he tipped into a customer's coal house; in the warmer months, the same large, brown carthorse would pull a diminutive ice cream cart. Whichever role he was playing, Mr B appeared somewhat unhappy, but that is only when compared with the boundless good nature we children possessed during the summer holidays. How could anyone not share our joy? Although there must have been many a parent, usually a mother, who counted down the days to when school would start again.

To be fair, Mr B's seriousness was understandable when lifting hundredweight sacks of coal from the sides of the wagon onto his shoulders, albeit protected by a special, tough leather waistcoat, some spilling down his neck and, in our case, catching on the rather low lintel of the lane door, causing him to duck and make even more unwelcome effort. He was pretty good at grunting during this exercise as well he may.

His waistcoat was of a type worn by all coalmen. Without arms, it was a very long waistcoat, especially elongated at the back; and in the front it was of jacket length, fastened right up to the neck with a leather strap. It was very robust which was essential if his clothes and his shoulders were not to suffer.

He would turn around at our coal house door and let the one hundredweight sack drop off his back and grunt, inhaling several deep breaths of coal dust. Each empty sack was then placed on the ground in our yard to be counted before paying in cash.

Coalman and wagon

All houses had coal houses. Since coal was the only fuel for heating water as well as heating rooms, it was used in large quantities and every house needed it. They were built into a house as part of its architecture, just as essential as having a toilet, which were usually outside too. The fuel being outside, it was an uncomfortable chore to have to go into the yard in winter to fill the coal bucket, which was always kept on the hearth of the fireplace. Most homes used the cheaper bituminous coal, a soft variety that gave off a lot of smoke and sulphur. It had, however, the advantage that it caught fire quickly. Its great disadvantage was that it contributed significantly to winter smog and was not helpful to those suffering from lung conditions either. But as with many things to which we become accustomed, the smell of sulphurous coal was a not an unpleasant signature smell. Even these days, if I smell the smoke of a coal fire it brings back strong memories.

Mr B retained this air of general suffering and penance when dispensing ice cream from his white cart in the summer, his mood seeming very misplaced. This was especially poignant since he had a polished brass bell on his brightly painted ice cream cart, mounted beneath an arch on the front of it. I always thought that the use of this bell must alleviate even the most depressed of service providers; but it was not so with Mr B. We rarely heard his bell in action, except for his entry into our back lane, when he rang it loudly. Mothers then dug frantically into their cluttered purses, and we ran into the lane with a bowl, or, if we paid more, we could buy ice cream sandwiched between two wafers.

We often asked him to ring his bell, but he stubbornly refused or just ignored us. After all, he was a big man and he may - this is my conjecture - have been a little embarrassed at acting the part of an ice cream man enclosed within such a highly decorated vehicle. Perhaps he felt that coal was his rightful dominion and this chilled cream luxury, dispensed to children, was somewhat beneath him. His refusal to ring his bell may also have been his way of showing his jealousy of us children, and even of ordinary folk, who didn't carry the burdens of business he clearly had. We lucky people could buy ice cream and go into our houses and enjoy it, whereas he was condemned to roam the lanes behind his large horse, perhaps for ever, as the Flying Dutchman of the ice cream trade.

I used to like having wafers: not only were they more portable than a bowl and spoon, they had an end point which was fun in itself. Making sure we didn't squeeze the wafer too much so that we retained the ice cream, we could end up, if we were skilled at it, with a miniature wafer at the end, which could be swallowed whole, the wafer being saturated by then with ice cream: soggy, yet still retaining some separation between our fingers and the cream.

Mr B's summer cart is worthy of close scrutiny. All white, with the rims of its white wheels decorated with a thin red line and the spokes of the wheels also in red, it was quite an attractive vehicle. But it sagged severely, especially at the rear. This was intentional, because then the driver-cum-ice cream salesman was able to step into it without any climbing. But the very low back, coupled with a necessarily higher front to accommodate the large horse, meant that it had a strange appearance, as though it was either about to take off, or simply collapse.

Mr B drove the cart from the same position from which he dispensed ice cream: from the centre of it, the reins of the horse passing through brass rings in the archway at the front. He entered through a very small, narrow door at the back and on either side of him would be two chilled tubs containing the ice cream. The tubs were immersed in ice, which he probably got from the fish warehouse at the docks.

Each galvanised tub was circular, with a round lid, in the middle of which was a brass knob. Dispensing ice cream into a bowl, he used a brass spoon, but dispensing the product into a wafer meant an altogether more complex implement. This was a clever device which stood in a small zinc bucket of water.

It was a hollow rectangle made of brass, standing on the top of a handle, which, when squeezed, would send the inner base of the rectangle upwards, so pushing out the contents. To begin, he had to place a wafer into the rectangle, fill it with ice cream, then add an upper wafer, before squeezing the handle. This always seemed to give so much more added value than offering up a bowl and having a blob of Mrs B's rich ice cream plopped into it.

Although Mr B and his odd ice cream cart were interesting, it was his horse which always attracted me. Like all horses it had an attractive smell and its coat shone. It was huge and vastly overpowered for its gentle summer task. I suppose it was impressive for that reason. It never seemed bad tempered in spite of waiting patiently at each stop. I could admire the huge muscles of the animal which seemed at odds with its gentle nature. Why would such a powerful animal agree to drag carts and to stop and start at Mr B's command? Why didn't it try to escape?

It, like all horses at the time, wore blinkers, but it was still possible to see its eyes. They seemed to be looking out at the world from deep within some other world of its own. I thought it a little cruel that it wore blinkers but the horse had the last laugh, for it had a stubbornness all its own. You could deduce this from the fact that such a beautiful ice cream cart would, for some strange reason, only drive around the back lanes and never along the open streets. This was because the horse refused to follow routes when delivering ice cream other than those it used when delivering coal.

Furthermore, to add to Mr B's frustration, it only stopped at the exact addresses where he normally delivered coal. But not all those having coal would want ice cream and not all those wanting ice cream would get it. So Mr B had to occasionally hire one of us to hold the reins of his horse at an address which didn't have coal in order to ensure it had ice cream, whilst he talked to an animal which ignored customers and only understood addresses. Our reward was more ice cream. And it was wonderful, creamy stuff.

As if this treat were not enough, I sometimes had a second reward from my grandfather if I followed Mr B (actually his horse) and scooped into a bucket any horse droppings that plopped onto the lane. My grandfather was a keen gardener who thought this was wonderful stuff to collect and to place in an old bin with water on top with which to water his roses. I was never too sure about the attractiveness of it, especially when it was fresh and still at body temperature, exhibiting an odour and a vapour that I can still smell. The shovel I used was the same one kept beside the living room fire to add coal to it.

I can't claim to have struck up a close rapport with this horse or its driver, but I did become quite attached to both of them. This was because, of a summer's evening, I occasionally cycled over to Grange Farm and helped to hang up and clean the leather and brass harnesses which it wore. The whole process of removing it, cleaning it, brushing down the horse and watering it probably took about an hour. Then it would be walked across Clive Street and under the railway bridge to its field, the first field on the left after the station.

All of Penarth Road was then fields and open countryside which was our green belt around an otherwise brick and tarmac world. I knew the horse's field as the Fair Field, being the occasional venue for a fair. I think Mr B may have had some connection with fairground people and gypsies, because they often camped there.

The horse, without its harness would look rather naked but it also looked like a real horse as it ran into its field and sometimes kicked its heels into the air with delight. The contrast between the innocent, happy horse and the heavy steps of its owner was stark, as he and I walked back to the Grange Farm. Even the way he trudged home, his hobnails scraping the pavement, seemed to confirm that he was truly fed up with his lot, be it coal or ice cream.

He hardly ever spoke, not a word, just grunted and coughed and spat. He was lost it seemed, in an awful world of coal and dark thoughts. I don't know why I liked him so much, but I did.

CHAPTER FOUR

Boots and Clogs

People often stayed in the same job for life. My grandfather, John, retired after forty-seven years of service at the gasworks, where his father had also worked. He had various jobs there during that time, beginning as an indentured apprentice at the age of fourteen and then continuing as a journeyman until he took up his first adult appointment at the age of eighteen as a steam engine driver. He went on to qualify as a crane driver and eventually was in charge of the pump house, where gas was pumped into the gas mains of the city and electricity was generated for the works.

A life-long job and the stability it offered was something most people wished for and it was quite normal in our area. Changing jobs was unnecessary if the work was there and it provided a steady, foreseeable income for a family. Why change?

Promotion and pay were based not only on competence and experience but as a reward for sticking at it, persevering in the same job with the same company over time. Stickability, constancy and dedicated service were valued character traits to employers.

The habits acquired from such jobs imprinted themselves on the character of the people involved. It affected their behaviour, their values and contributed to their satisfaction. They wore these slowly-constructed characteristics just as they wore clothes. Work also showed in their physical characteristics. Rough, calloused hands spoke of continued hard labour. Pale faces spoke of night shift working, or men who hardly saw the light of day from within dark cavernous buildings.

Sometimes injuries were evident, such as burns from the steel works, or broken bones from accidents in transport industries. Eyesight could weaken or eyes be damaged by heat and flame. This

Furnace worker

was known as 'flash eye' or 'furnace eye'. Hearing often suffered from the sheer noise of industry.

Little was known and little concern was shown about such things. Both workers and employers labelled injuries and a general deterioration in health as the natural risk of certain jobs, the most risky being rewarded by higher pay or specific danger money.

Working clothes would also offer broad clues as to someone's occupation, from the clothes they wore and the hours they kept.

Employers did not always provide working clothes, employees had to wear their own clothes. This meant that clothes were varied and interesting. We can see from photographs of the time that many men wore suits to work, even when engaged in manual work, although those in the heaviest and most dangerous industries usually made themselves special protective clothing, such as a leather apron for working in foundries, heavy manufacturing plants, or brick making.

One of our neighbours was a signalman, always working night shifts in the same signal box for over forty years, so we rarely saw him and when we did he was always pale. Another neighbour was a foundry worker, who wore wooden clogs and leather chaps over his

Tapping a furnace

trousers to guard against the dangers of molten metal. Many men in Grangetown worked in such industries and were seen on the streets with their own brands of workwear.

Footwear was a definite give-away as to where someone worked. Few wore shoes; most wore heavy boots, often studded, and even wooden clogs. Heavy leather boots were expensive and had to last, so they were protected by rows of steel studs on the soles and heels, which, when they wore away could be replaced, keeping the basic boot for further wear. And what a beautiful noise they made on the pavements! Here comes someone in a seriously important job; he strides with confidence in those steel-soled boots. Listen as a group of men come down the street, their boots striking sparks from the York Stone pavement.

Clogs were also studded in this way, but usually had a rim of steel, rather like a horse-shoe, fitted to the outer edge of the sole and with a steel plate at the heel. Wooden clogs may be thought of as uncomfortable, but many men, including my grandfather, maintained that they were the only footwear for heavy work and were actually good for the feet. Bearing in mind that socks were generally made (often by hand) from thick wool, the feet didn't suffer from sweating if clogs were worn – unlike when wearing enclosed boots. Thin, elasticated socks weren't available then and thick knitted woollen socks were bad for the feet, especially in summer. Most clogs were made by hand, to measure, and fitted perfectly.

Men working in dusty environments, such as in the brick works, or simply where there was a lot of dirt and perhaps mud, protected their legs by using straps tightened around their trousers, just below the knee. Underneath they would wear long woollen socks to above the knee and with this precautionary overlap they were well protected against dirt. Many houses didn't have baths so people often bathed only once a week. Being able to just wash one's calves was a great help in keeping clean.

Almost all heavy industries ran continuously, with the men working shifts. Most shift workers were allocated a more or less permanent shift; they might be, for example, 'afternoon men' (working 2pm until 10pm) or they might be on 'nights'. Some worked these same shifts for many years and seemed to like it that way. Stability was a comfort; but it may have taken a toll on their health. The relatively modern rotating shift system would have probably been much better for them.

In the morning, in our street, some time before six o'clock, we would hear the steel studs of the early shift going to work and just after 6:30 we'd hear their fellow workers coming home off the night shift. The steel studs of their boots or clogs would make quite a racket, always accompanied by conversations and laughter. It happened every day, even Sunday; it was unvarying and reassuring, like hearing the chimes of Big Ben.

The sound of boots on pavements announced that all was well; the world was turning as it always had done. Work, there was a-plenty at this time, in the 40s and 50s. To be unemployed was almost unknown and was a source of shame, even if there was a good reason, such as having a disability due to the war.

Sundays, with the exception of shift workers in essential industries, was a day of silence. Nothing moved. Buses were rarities and only a skeleton service on the railways was provided. Quietness was everywhere and people made a very deliberate effort not to do anything noisy.

This silence was healing; people even talked more quietly if they were out on the street, respecting others' need for rest and worship. As children we were not allowed to play noisily and certainly not in the street. Any games were restricted to back lanes and they had to be quiet.

Sunday was a wonderful institution. It punctuated our week and, just as a punctuation mark inserts a pause and gives meaning to a sentence, the pause worked likewise on the weeks of our lives. It was a reference point, a different day, when work stopped. We have lost this very precious day and missed the point it taught us: that man needs quietness, recuperation and time to have thoughts of a higher order other than just work. Of course, once cars became affordable,

St Paul's Church

some families would set off for the seaside or the hills, but most families went to church or chapel.

Sunday was a day on which everyone gathered their strength for the week ahead. I went to the Baptist Chapel in Clive Street at eleven o'clock and then, after a huge Sunday lunch, I returned at 2:30pm with my mother and brother for Sunday School. People dressed in their Sunday best of course and tucked their Bibles under their arms as they walked, not drove, to church. To drive to church or chapel was seen as cheating and perhaps showing off.

My father never went to church or chapel, but my mother and grandmother did, although to different establishments. My grandmother, being C of E, went to Saint Paul's Church, Paget Street, shown on the previous page. I didn't mind going to chapel and even enjoyed the Sunday routine most of the time, but sometimes, on a nice summer's day, I would rather have been in a park, playing. One Sunday, in just such weather, I suggested to my younger brother, Brian, that since Mam was not going to chapel that afternoon, she'd never know if we went to the park instead. But she did know! The Sunday School teacher asked her the following week why we hadn't been there. I didn't do it again.

Clive Street Baptist Chapel

* * *

As we grew older, my brother and I attended Sunday services more reluctantly. In fact, Sundays themselves gradually became less strict as the years rolled on. For me, being fascinated by jazz music, there was a new temptation for me to stay at home. My father, who was a very good dance band pianist, had a number of friends with whom he liked to play. A friend, at the end of the street, played fabulous lead guitar (he was a carpenter and even made his own guitar); his sons, B and G also played lead and rhythm guitars respectively. B was especially good at country and western and all three of them were professional level players. B later created a number of country and western groups and made several records. They were very successful.

Sometimes, they would all congregate in our front room around the piano, with another friend who brought a simple snare drum. They even had a bass player once. The front room floor would rock on its weak floorboards to the sound of fabulous jazz classics. *Limehouse Blues, Ain't Misbehavin', Avalon,* and many of Django Reinhard's best pieces. All this on a Sunday too!

Our weak floorboards were a source of chronic concern in our house, it having been built over a marsh that was still damp. Joists and floorboards simply rotted away and were replaced a few times. As for the effect the marsh had on our health, I never really investigated it. One thing I do know, however, is that the house never entirely lost its slightly musty smell, something that I became more sensitive about when inviting teenage friends who lived in better houses, ones not built on a marsh. My grandparents, especially, were always keen to open up the windows and doors to air the place.

There was a Roman Catholic family several doors down who ensured their place in heaven by their very regular attendance at church. In the summer, with our front room window wide open and the noise of people making music leaking out, the family would (I swear it!) slow down as they passed the window in order to give us a withering stare of saintly disapproval.

My grandmother played the harmonium, but only on Sundays - thank heavens! It was a large instrument, requiring significant physical strength to simultaneously pump the bellows with the feet and operate the 'swell' and loudness levers with the knees, besides pulling out all sorts of ivory-tipped organ stops. As she became older and less athletic, we were rescued from the doleful, asthmatic wheeze of this instrument and the hymns she used to play. Whether she felt better for giving the thing a rest I don't know, but, frankly, we did.

My brother and I used to try and get some kind of sound out of it, one of us peddling with our hands and the other pulling out various stops and

Harmonium

peculiar mechanical appendages to see what would happen. But we never succeeded in generating anything like an attractive or even recognisable sound. We assumed that the Victorians, who invented the thing, were basically pretty depressed and miserable and used the instrument to drive home their negative view of life. It was a real spoiler of a thing.

If a householder who had one of these things didn't feel particularly sad one day, they soon would once they tried playing it. It seemed to be the anti-matter version of a piano. Not only the weird wheezy sound it made would dampen any spirit but also the way it looked. It was heavy, in weight and appearance. It almost looked at you with a frown of disapproval. Ideal for a wet Sunday, I suppose.

*　*　*

Back in the gasworks pump house, my grandfather was in charge of the huge steam-driven pumps that had to maintain the gas pressure in the mains and inflate the large gas holders, which are a feature of every gasworks. This was a very responsible job and an indoor one; it held fewer dangers than moving around the works in an engine, although the gas being pumped was of course explosive and the steam engines powering them needed to be treated with respect.

When promoted to this work, he was able to change his working clothes, from wearing heavy overalls and clogs, which he then kept for gardening, to wearing leather boots and lighter clothing because of the heat.

His work in the pump house was something I used to admire and I visited him at work from time to time, which I then felt, and still do, to be a privilege. Young boys often aspired to be engineers, to be master of a steam engine of some sort. To be able to leave the world of childhood play and be admitted to the serious adult world of work in such a busy, noisy, dangerous, smelly place as the gasworks was a dream come true.

Sometimes, for reasons that were not clear to me, he had to work very long hours and on these exceptional occasions, when he may not come home for meals for a day or so, I would take his hot lunch to him on my bike. I would have to stop at the watchman's hut of course and ask permission to enter the works (little did they know

I often visited the place without them knowing) and they would direct me to his pump house.

What struck me the first time I did this was that as soon as I mentioned who I was looking for, the men in the gate hut all knew him. It appeared that my grandfather was well known and therefore I was recognised too.

Thinking back on it, wandering unaccompanied through such a dangerous place at such a young age, was actually a pretty outrageous thing to do, by today's standards. I had to not only penetrate the cavernous works buildings but also cross railway tracks, avoid shunting steam engines and steer well clear of the red-hot coke ovens. If I survived this, I then had to climb a high-level gantry and cross over sheds full of dangers, including ducking under the girders of a passing crane.

One such route meant crossing over vats of molten tar, the fumes from which could intoxicate quite quickly. Walking past red-hot coke ovens, which every so often would discharge their glowing contents into wagons for cooling, accompanied by an explosion of steam and heat, was also pretty dangerous.

The sights, smells, steam, smoke and noise were so exciting! Cranes rolled overhead on gantries, lifting and transporting coal and coke; trams of hot tar and slag were being shunted in and out of dark, smoky sheds. Coke, glowing red-hot, would be pushed out of a retort into a steel wagon and sometimes doused with water, issuing vast clouds of steam accompanied by explosions. What a fascinating place to work, I thought. I was so proud that my grandfather held the position he did.

Coke oven ready for discharge

The pump house itself was a high, well-lit hall, with a polished red-tiled floor. It was immaculately clean and tidy. My grandfather tended the three mammoth pumping machines, always with his oilcan and rag to hand. He wore either faded or pale blue overalls, always with a tie and waistcoat beneath. I remember him looking very smart and that his overalls had been ironed with a crease down each trouser leg. Smartness counted even working in the pump house.

There were three huge gas pumps, partly sunk into pits, with a polished brass safety rail around them. Each would thunder round at an enormous speed, their dark green flywheels spinning, being driven by polished steel pistons which churned rapidly back and fore as they compressed the gas for the city of Cardiff. They were driven by steam engines, which were especially interesting. Hot and full of innate power, they were to be feared and yet held an irresistible fascination. I suppose that this mixed characteristic of danger and utility is what made steam power so impressive and so exciting: it was to be feared as well as appreciated.

My grandfather and his mate had a set of well-used, steel lockers at the remote end of the pump house, in the centre of the far wall. These were where men looking after the machines put their clothes and kept their chipped enamel mugs and plates.

In front of the lockers was a scrubbed deal table with a bench on the locker side and comfortable-looking old arm chairs at either end. Here, my grandfather and his assistant would sit for a break or

Gas Works

meals. His newspaper was often on the table together with his glasses, so he must have had the time to sit and read occasionally. But they certainly couldn't smoke in such a dangerous place.

Presenting my grandfather safely with his lunch was something I remember doing with great pride, not least of all for having safely navigated all the dangers en route and having found his place of work at all. He then showed me round the various engines and some smaller ones at the side which generated electricity.

Amongst all the impressions of my grandfather's pump house, the most striking was how clean and well-tended everything was. Brass shone, paint glistened and of course there was the lovely, all-pervasive smell of hot oil. I had to wait whilst he ate his meal and make the dangerous return journey, checking in at the lodge on my way out, so they knew I'd survived.

***

We began this chapter considering working clothes and footwear. Not only men wore boots and clogs. My grandfather's (Irish) widowed mother, Sarah-Ann, also known as Granny Noyes who lived in Oakley Street, also wore clogs. She wore a sack apron and kept her hair tightly controlled under a hair net whenever I saw her. She was quite a character. We didn't see her very often, although my grandfather used to pop in and see her on his way back from work when he could.

I have a vivid memory of her and her small house. She was small, roughly spoken and lived mostly in a poorly lit living room at the rear of the house, with a scullery at the back of the room. She didn't seem to use the rest of the house except for her bedroom. The living room was heated by a fire in a huge, cast iron range, beneath a deep mantle shelf covered in a red chenille cloth, about 10 inches of which hung down over the shelf and was

Victorian living room

edged in little balls of the same material. The photograph below shows a similar fireplace but a rather bare one.

Beneath the mantle cloth, two brass rails, one in front of the other, were used for drying clothes. A tall brass fender with strange knobs on either corner and elaborate cut-outs on its front and sides kept all the ash and cinders away from the one small mat in front of the fire. One day, I strayed into the other downstairs room in the front of the house and had a fright. I remember the dismal, dark room very well: it contained no furniture at all, had bare boards and piled against the wall in the alcove to the left of the fireplace were planks of wood.

The darkness was heavy. The window was covered by the dirtiest of net curtains. It looked as though the house had been cleared of furniture and was ready for demolition. Why it should have been in such a state and so scary I don't know, but I know my brother shared the same sense of nervousness about the room. Most houses in those days were deliberately dark in common with the fashion of the day, including our own, but this one had a darkness and a dinginess which was memorable. How could someone live in such a place, I wondered? There seemed to be absolutely no comfort in it at all and it was neglected as though it didn't matter.

In our house, the use of Victorian-style, heavy drapes across the windows (also beneath the archway in the hall) together with wooden Venetian blinds ensured that little direct sunlight entered. This was not only fashionable, but also practical. Furniture, both wooden and fabric covered, suffered from damage and fading if the sun struck them. French polish, for example, soon crackles under the sun. Moquette, the covering of soft furniture, used simple, organic dyes which would fade.

The Forge Inn

Granny Noyes smoked a short clay pipe, badly burned around the bowl and with a stem stained with nicotine. She loved her drink apparently. In those days, the pub on The Square (the Forge Inn), as it was known, used to sell gin on draught from a small barrel in what was known as the 'snug'. This was a tiny room mainly used by women; and I suppose she, like many others, would have gone there with a small jug or other container and bought some. Beer too was sold like this, as was milk. The photograph shows the Forge Inn at the end of her street.

A dairy was situated near The Square, which received churns of milk straight from neighbouring farms, bottled it and delivered it to our doorsteps. Many liquids were not sold in containers, as they are now; one had to have one's own container and go to a retailer who had bought whatever it was in bulk and who would decant it into one's container. This applied to paraffin, for example. Ironmongers, of which there were a few, would keep the stuff in the back of the shop in large steel drums and fill whatever container you had brought for it. Many houses used paraffin heaters to take the chill off bedrooms in the winter.

Besides milk, beer, spirits and paraffin, vinegar and lubricating oil were also dispensed this way. Having no pre-packed containers meant there was no container to throw away, as we do now.

Granny Noyes fell ill when I was very young and came to our house to be nursed. She occupied a bed behind the front room door. It was a very high bed, I remember, as all beds were in those days. Mattresses with interior springing had not been invented and so the main wooden frame of the bed, to which the headboard and footboard were attached, carried a further frame on which various springs were stretched. Then, on top of that, a feather mattress was laid. Feather mattresses could be very comfortable and warm and took up the shape of those sleeping in them. They therefore had to be shaken up from time to time to refresh their shape, otherwise hollows would form and those could be uncomfortable.

I mention these details, because to a small boy, as I was then, trying to look at someone in bed meant that it was a difficult job unless one had a small stool on which to stand. When I looked in on Granny Noyes, therefore, I looked straight into her face, rather than down on her. And this was rather scary, ill and frail that she was.

Eventually, she died when I was four. She was the first dead person I'd seen. A Funeral Director was not always used for preparing the dead for burial, often the family did it themselves. So my grandmother and mother took care of the body, washing it and preparing it for burial.

Funerals often took place from the home, not from so-called chapels of rest. Granny Noyes was placed in a coffin, which was left open for a few days whilst visitors came and went, offering their respects to her and the family. All blinds and curtains were drawn, not only in our house, but in the neighbours' houses too. This was always done as a sign of respect. This respect was echoed on the streets, where men and boys would remove their hats whenever a funeral passed by, whether they knew the deceased or not. This is in stark contrast to today when a funeral is often treated as a nuisance by other road users.

On the day of the funeral, a service was held in the front room and the coffin was passed through the front window out into the street and onto a horse-drawn hearse. The window was used because it was not possible to turn the coffin in the narrow passage of the house. This was a very frequent method of exiting this world. She was buried in Ely cemetery, quite near the boundary fence. We went there fairly frequently to look after her grave afterwards.

I really don't know why Granny Noyes wore a sack apron all the time. I always felt as though she had been engaged in some really rough work whenever I saw her with it. Many people used sacking for protection against the weather, when it would be worn over the shoulders, or on washing day as an apron. My grandmother had one set aside for just this purpose each Monday when it was washing day and my mother wore a red rubber one against the water.

Washing clothes by hand or with a rudimentary machine was a messy business. Mangles were the only high tech household gadget to aid the drying of clothes and they required quite a bit of muscle power to operate them, when squeezing bedding dry, for example. Many a finger was squashed in a mangle too! Some were mounted on an electrically heated boiler, but the electricity supply of most houses wouldn't be able to provide enough power for that; so water was heated by a coal fire with a boiler at the back of it, from which the hot water rose to a storage tank in the house.

Workmen, such as those digging the roads, also wore sacks. They always had one to hand in case of bad weather. They weren't supplied with weatherproof clothing so sacks were worth a lot to them in keeping them dry. These men were navvies, the word coming from navigators, those who were employed on roads, canals and railways, and they were a race apart. Very tough, very rough and often of Irish extraction, they were fascinating men and ones to be somewhat wary of.

I remember a nearby road was having its tramlines taken up and replaced by tarmac. Navvies, in gangs, were the sole source of power, except for steam rollers. The men seemed to be able to work continuously without rest and wield a pick or a shovel all day long, no matter what the weather. These giants of men would smash up the road surface and dig down into its foundations in torrential rain or blazing sun without the aid of pneumatic drills, just with a pick.

They worked in gangs and always set up a base with a green canvas hut or tent near their place of operations. This would be their shelter where their dry clothes and tools would be kept and they'd use it for taking breaks, making tea and having food. And what food! It was usually meat, bought at a nearby butcher's and cooked on their shovels over a flaming brazier. No need for vegetables or other niceties – just steaks, huge ones.

I witnessed similar culinary expertise later in life when supervising the construction of electricity pylons across the top of mountains in mid Wales. Machines were unable to access the boggy sites so the navvies were called in to dig the most enormous foundations by hand, cooking their steaks on their shovels, washed down with bottles of beer.

A fire brazier at the work site, outside the green tent, was kept burning day and night; not only for cooking, crude that it was, or for heating water for the gallons of tea they drank; but also to keep the watchman warm during the night. Unlike today, when machines do the digging and can be simply locked up at night, years ago hand tools were used, lots of them, and they had to be guarded. Additionally, the watchman had to make sure the red oil-filled safety lanterns were kept lit along the roadside. These were hung on poles and ropes around an excavation so that people and vehicles could avoid it.

The lanterns were red metal boxes with round red glass lenses on all four sides. On the top, a crude metal strip was bent into a hook which served to carry them and to hook them onto things. Small, oil wick burners flickered inside and had to be regularly topped up with paraffin. On windy nights they tended to blow out, which was not very helpful.

I've no idea where these navvies stayed when they travelled from job to job; but when they were in an area there were often fights at chucking-out time at the pubs. The Catholic Club at the top of our street was a top attraction for these largely Irish labourers and became a focal point for fighting.

I can remember many a fracas of a Saturday night as fights spilled out onto the pavement. But I can never remember anyone being badly hurt. Boxing was a sport which seemed to be pretty prevalent in Grangetown and my grandfather was a keen follower of it. I think the locals who trained in boxing sometimes fancied their chances against the navvies who looked quite unable to do much except dig trenches; but the locals soon discovered how hard they could punch as well as dig.

The fights were usually sorted out amicably, or if not, a policeman on his bike would suddenly appear and do the sorting out himself. By this I mean he would sometimes physically sort them out. Most policemen at that time were recruited for their size, I think, for they always looked huge.

We were visited once by a policeman whom my grandfather knew and when he appeared at the front door of the house, he could only just get in by ducking his head. Bearing in mind that Victorian houses like ours had high ceilings and tall doors to match, it must have meant that he was getting on for seven feet tall. You didn't mess about with policemen in those days, who had free rein to discipline people as they thought best, including children like us.

Undoubtedly, the best part of watching road works in progress was seeing the working of the steamrollers. They were not only impressive for their weight and power, but also for the noises they made. The clanking of the chains on the front roller and the noise of the hollow rear ones made a lovely sound. A few of these mammoth machines were still steam-driven although they were very rare.

We used to toss copper coins, usually halfpennies, in front of the roller to see how flat it would squash them, but they were hardly touched; they were simply pushed into the still-soft tarmac. The same was not to be said of placing a coin on a railway line.

If you were able to get onto a line used by the huge express locomotives, then your penny would be well and truly squashed into an oval about 2 inches at its longest part. This was strictly illegal of course and highly dangerous, but great fun. There was a point between the Cardiff railway sheds and the central station where the fence was broken and allowed us lads to get onto the line.

I had ample opportunity for watching all this exciting work going on in the streets, as the old tramlines were dug up and the roads prepared for a new mode of transport, the trolley bus.

CHAPTER FIVE
Early Schooldays

Grangetown Board School, 1884

Many of our values originated from and were reinforced by the clubs and institutions to which we belonged – scouts, cubs, boys' brigade, youth clubs, etc. But it was our sojourn in school that planted most of the seeds of behaviour. I began school when I was five, at

Grangetown Council School. This is a photograph of it when it opened in 1884.

It was originally named the Grangetown Board School, the name coming from the Education Act of 1870 which provided free education for all children in England and Wales, managed by elected boards of trustees.

The Act allowed voluntary schools to continue if they wished, but established a system of school boards, under the local authorities. They were tasked with building and managing schools in areas where they were needed. They were elected bodies paid for out of the rates or community tax.

Unlike religious schools, board schools were initially non-denominational, but much later they were encouraged to practice a Christian agenda with hymn singing and Bible readings. In the 1950s radio broadcasts of worship were established, taking place each Friday morning and relayed to many schools, including my own.

The boards could set the budget and the curriculum of schools and could determine the ages at which all children in their area should attend. They also determined the calendar of the school year. To maintain standards, they employed school inspectors who would report both to the heads of schools and the boards. Discipline and attendance were both treated seriously, absentees being identified and visited at their homes.

Previously education, even at primary level, was fee-paying, albeit a few pence a week. This meant that the poorest families could not always afford to have their children attend school. There were numerous instances of this in Grangetown from Victorian times to the 20th century. Non-payment of fees was especially prevalent when the wage-earning man in the house was ill or out of work. Some boards provided charity relief for such situations.

Voluntary free schools, often supported by chapels, were established and very early in its history there was a notable one in Grangetown run by a Mr Buck, a lay preacher. Many schools were run by religious organisations, many of which continue to this day. In Victorian times, it was often middle class women who not only sponsored charitable or private schools but also taught in them. These were known as 'lady schools'.

The school I attended resembled a church rather than a school. It had very tall, vaulted ceilings of stout timber beams, large fireplaces, high-up windows (to make it impossible for children to look out and be distracted) and huge gothic arches, all contributing to the impression that it was a cathedral of learning. Everything was varnished and brown; the tiles on the walls were brown (although in two shades: brown and darker brown) and it was all rather sombre. The school was built in the early 1880s and had all the appearance to me of something rather splendid.

The buildings provided space for three ages of pupils: the primary school at one end; the junior school at the other, and in the centre a large girls' secondary modern school; large in the sense that it had three storeys to it.

I found school absolutely thrilling. In primary school we were taught to read, count, spell and write; to play and to question. Joined-up writing and serious arithmetic followed later. My first two years there I was taught along traditional lines and really enjoyed the structured, disciplined approach. And good progress was made, I believe. At least I began reading and writing and all seemed well.

The primary school end of the building today

And then, in the last year of primary school, the government decided that children shouldn't have structured learning, but should learn through playing. They should only learn what they were interested in and only when they felt like it.

Suddenly, when we returned from summer holidays that year, the school buildings had been transformed. The huge, glazed, wooden partitions which separated one classroom from another, were folded back and the whole school was open to us to wander around as we wished and to do whatever we wanted. Sand pits had been imported; lots of water was on hand with which to splash around and play; blackboards had been wheeled out of the way and play blocks and other toys were there.

Neither I, nor my parents, liked this idea at all. Just what, exactly, were we children supposed to be doing? Where was the syllabus and the objectives which we hoped to reach? What kind of school report was going to be written at the end of it? Parents were not at all happy.

Groups of them gathered in the playground at the end of school, endlessly questioning the teachers who seemed to be just as clueless as they were. We pupils too felt at a loose end. There was nothing to get our teeth into. I could play with sand, water and mud whenever I liked and did! Why had they abandoned us? Parents called it 'playing with sand and water' and this is all it really was.

I mention this, not only because it was an upsetting change for me, but it signalled the start of decades of fiddling about with our education system which is still far from over.

There were two things, however, which stick in my memory concerning this primary school period of my life when I was about five or six years old: one was a period in the afternoons when we were encouraged to sleep and the other was the games we used to play in the yard at break time.

At three o'clock each afternoon, the youngest children had to go into the largest classroom, where a suitable number of steel-framed, canvas-covered folding beds had been laid out. They were dark green in colour and very uncomfortable. You were supposed to

Playing a game of marbles

sleep on them on command. Needless to say, we just looked at each other from beneath half-closed eyelids and smiled, pretending to sleep and looking forward to the glass of orange juice we were given afterwards.

Our smiles were best expressed at playtime. The most exciting game we used to play was 'chariots'. Two friends would stand alongside each other and link arms behind each other's backs. A charioteer would then climb onto their backs and all three would charge head on at another 'chariot'. This was actually crazy, many a bloody nose resulted, but great fun to see which pair would be the overall winners.

We also played marbles (also called 'allies', deriving from alabaster from which the earliest marbles were made). The corners of the yard, where there was more likelihood of some peace and quiet, were filled with chalk circles on the ground, showing where games had been played. This became quite serious at times. We even used to play on the way home, from pavement to road to gutter. On one occasion, a rather dirty and unpleasant chap called B decided he liked my marbles better than his and decided to beat me up and steal them. Being of a stoic and very robust character I wasn't going to let that happen – so I gave them to him!

When I was seven, going on eight, we moved, thank heaven, away from playing with sand and water and into the junior school. The first class was in a concrete, so-called 'temporary' classroom which is still there now, almost seventy years later. Our teacher was the best: Miss G. It was she who taught us 'real' writing and arithmetic.

She was a large, warm-hearted lady who also liked discipline, which is a healthy combination. We loved her and all wanted to be her pet. This position was gained by doing good work and showing a steady application, and was rewarded by being allowed access to her stationery cupboard or to clean the blackboard.

The cupboard was at the left (as we looked at it) of the blackboard and what an interesting blackboard it was! Part of it was ruled permanently in blue and red lines for joined-up writing exercises, whilst another part was ruled off in squares for arithmetic. On first seeing this I remember thinking that this is going to be serious stuff at last; it was in her class that I first used a pen, ink and blotting paper.

They were actually nice pens to use although some were quite scratchy. All pens had to be handed in at the end of the day, so we were never certain whether we'd get someone else's damaged one the next day.

The photograph right is not of my classroom but has been chosen to show the style of desks, especially the teacher's high desk, and the holes in them for china inkwells. The tall teachers' desks were in several classrooms and were probably the original ones provided when the school was first opened in 1884.

1950s classroom

Once a week the ink monitor would go into the stationery cupboard, get a large bottle of ink and go around the desks filling the small, white china inkwells. Occasionally, someone would somehow manage to spill an entire inkwell and the results would be more or less impossible to erase and many a desk carried the evidence in blue or black patches over the top of it and even inside it. The area around the ink well was always covered in ink because it was almost impossible to dip those pens into an inkwell without dripping a little.

Ink blots on our work were also something we had to avoid and it was very easy, after dipping the pen into the ink well, to drip some onto your work as you brought the pen back to your exercise book. Neatness in all we did was important and learning how to work neatly in an ink medium was something that a minority of children just didn't seem to be able to manage at that age. Our fingers would always show evidence of our working in ink, but some people seemed to get it over their clothes and even their faces.

Pen, ink and ruler

Next door, was another classroom just like ours, where another stream of children were taught, by a man who had very hairy hands, I remember, but whose name I cannot recall. His style was quite different and we weren't so keen on him. But each morning, the two classes would cram into his and we'd have a morning service of hymns and Bible readings.

One of the features of our temporary or 'annexed' classroom was that it was an island in the yard, adjacent to the wall of the school so that when standing up we could see the heads of people walking along the street. This partial contact with ordinary life was quite a change from the dark, high-ceilinged cathedral that had been our primary school. Any contact our teacher needed to make with other staff, notably the head teacher, often required either that she leave us and walk to the main building, or send a runner with a message. To be a runner was also a form of reward because you had a break in your lesson.

In common with most schools at that time, ours didn't have inside toilets. We had to dash across the yard to the outside loos, which were freezing in the winter. No hand basins were provided and the washing of hands after using the toilet only really came into common practice after a national epidemic of some sort. Significant numbers of children contracted the disease and we were all urged to wash our hands more often. An emergency national vaccination programme was undertaken to tackle the outbreak.

There was no gym in our primary or junior schools. Our monitored exercise consisted of the occasional exodus into the school yard on a suitably dry day to play with wooden hoops and balls. We were formed into teams and given woven coloured sashes to wear as our team colours. The hoops had to be rolled along or thrown up in the air, sometimes to each other.

This was in fact a much more gentle form of exercise than we usually engaged in when left to our own devices, so I never really saw the point of it; but it was a pleasant interlude from indoor lessons. We rarely had break cancelled even when it rained. We were able to play under a large shelter which was against one of the walls of the playground, although there was very little room if the whole school took shelter.

Those of us in the earliest forms were of course the youngest and began to realise that older kids played quite differently to us. We were still interested in running around a lot, hiding and seeking, pulling girls' plaited hair and so on. The older ones were more sullen and more interested in teasing; this applied especially to those in the final year, awaiting their fate when they eventually took the eleven-plus exam.

Miss G never used the cane but the teacher in our next (second year) class, Mr W, did. His classroom was in the main building. He was a very dapper and upright ex-army man, complete with a thin, pencil-line moustache and perfectly round glasses. After the war, many men were drafted into education to make good the numbers of teachers lost.

He was always on parade. Stiff and proper, his shoes were polished to a mirror shine as was his head: his Brylcreemed hair was brushed down to a flat, polished finish like shiny black plastic, but with a centre parting. His heavy, brogue shoes were tipped with steel on the heels, so that when he walked on the bare floorboards inside the school or even in the playground, his assertive presence was made clear. I'm sure he felt he was back in the army, determined to knock us rookies into shape and impart some discipline, which he did.

He wore tweed jackets and his collars were starched ones, like my grandfather wore. Because they were very stiff and sharp-edged, they had the effect (on all wearers) of ensuring the head was held up, eyes front, otherwise they could rub or even cut the wearer's neck. He had therefore developed the habit of regularly and suddenly pushing out his jaw, so as to free his neck from the collar's tight grip and sharp edges.

In the winter, he would add a light rust-coloured waistcoat to his brown tweed jacket, the latter having green leather patches on its elbows and cuffs. When arriving or leaving school, he would acknowledge none of the children, as he strode through the gates, eyes front, chin up, his tightly rolled umbrella swinging in syncopation with his army regulation strides. If it was not raining, he always folded his raincoat neatly so that it sat perfectly over one shoulder and stayed there. In the summer, his attire would be lightened somewhat to a pale brown lightweight jacket and no waistcoat; but he made up for this missing item by wearing a straw Panama when outside.

Shown below is the first storey of the school where we graduated from one classroom to the next, ending up sitting our eleven-plus examination in the room in the gable end of the building.

Upper storey of Grangetown School from St Fagans Street

Perhaps Mr W was aided in his ability to keep discipline by his physiognomy. He wore old fashioned black, circular glasses through which he would stare at us. His unflinching stare would be amplified by his lenses, within the dead centre of which his eyeballs shot forth a withering stare which was often accompanied by the cane thwacking the desk top. No pupil could ignore the shock of suddenly waking up to such a pair of laser eyes. I reckon that stare could open an oyster at 50 yards!

One of his favourite habits was taking the cane and tapping it continually on one of his trouser legs, beating the rhythm to which we chanted our times tables. It reminded us that he was our leader, like an officer with a swagger stick leading his troops into an imaginary battle.

Like an army officer, he knew us only by our surnames, which he pronounced clearly and succinctly. His was one of the few classes where total silence would reign during roll call (registration) each morning. No shuffling, murmuring of turning of heads. Arms would be folded and we sat up straight, announcing our presence with a clear voice. 'Speak up, boy, are you present or not?!'

He also kept one of the neatest and most colourful registers in the school: red stroke for absent, blue cross for ill, black stroke for present. Each day, the slope of the strokes alternated: Mondays they were from top right to bottom left; Tuesdays they were from top left to bottom right. That way, each pair of days made a triangular pattern that advanced across the page.

I must soften this picture of the regimental sergeant major *manqué* by remembering that he taught us music. We learned the French round of *Frère Jacques* and other classic songs, the rhythms all beaten out with military exactitude. He also played the piano, which revealed his softer side.

I always felt sorry for that piano. It was wheeled around the school, bouncing around on the uneven, worn floorboards for yet another bashing at the hands of teachers who felt that if the piano were played loudly, our background noises would be drowned out. They usually succeeded.

Each morning, first thing, it was time to recite our times tables followed by mental arithmetic. He was a great believer in learning by rote and I am grateful to him for it, because I learned much as a result of his discipline. Those children whose only aim in life seemed to be to disrupt lessons were very soon sorted out. He took no prisoners. Indeed, if repeated crimes were committed, the children (criminals) involved would be simply moved into a corner or into a row of desks reserved for the infringers and ignored.

He was a stickler for cleanliness and order in our work. Exercise books were to be kept clean and looked after; our hands were inspected routinely for cleanliness before beginning work. Writing was to be neat and well-formed. Even blotting paper (for we used ink pens with wooden handles and replaceable nibs) was to be used sparingly and kept flat and clean. Any blots, stains, smudges, crinkles and wobbly lines in our work were to be accounted for. Numbers were to be in perfect vertical columns, one under the other, none out of line.

His classroom was in the main building and was one of the largest. It had a fireplace, which we all faced, and which was at the back of his desk; in fact he had two desks. One was a desk about four or five feet high, on four long legs, at which he sat on a tall stool –

very Dickensian – and which was to the left as we faced it. From there, he could survey the whole class with a withering glance. It was from here he called the register in the morning.

Victorians were sticklers for posture, and having such a high desk meant that the teacher could not only see pupils easily, but could stand at it, something that was encouraged; sitting down to work was not always thought to be a good thing. In the same way, the seats of our desks were hard and plank-like, with backs that were vertical, so that it was impossible to slouch in them. These tall teachers' desks had sloping tops. It was frowned upon to stoop over one's desk; much better that the desk top be sloped, allowing the writer's back to remain straight. We were frequently told to straighten our backs, hold our heads up, stand up straight and sit up straight. 'How can you hope to learn anything, boy, when you're slouching?'. A question I have never yet been able to satisfactorily answer.

We children were treated like army recruits, which is not surprising bearing in mind the number of male teachers who had served in the war. Interestingly, the quasi-military culture I experienced in the school was not at all new. When the school first opened in the 1880s the Board employed an ex-drill sergeant major to impose discipline in the yard and corridors, requiring children to walk smartly, not to talk and to keep their heads up. He, together with the men who went out looking for absent children, imposed strict discipline throughout the young population of the school.

A further example of the emphasis on discipline was the name of the central corridor, which was labelled on the original architectural plans, as 'the boys' marching corridor'. Whenever we used it, for exiting the school or when simply moving from one classroom to another, we had to form up in single file, keeping to the left, and march, heads up swinging our arms as we went.

Mr W's second desk was more modern and used for dictating or reading. It was aligned on the central axis of the classroom which gave him rapid access to his stock of canes. They hung from pegs inside the door of the cupboards behind him and to the right of the fireplace. I retain these details because those children being disciplined had to get the instrument of their punishment from the said cupboard themselves: and I was not an exception.

His own insistence on high standards applied not only to our behaviour but also to the quality of his canes. He used to send one of us across the road to the corner shop, which stocked teachers' canes, to get some more when his wore out. Being of thin bamboo, if they were struck too hard on a desk or similar, the end would burst and become a set of fronds or strings, just waving about, like a stick of Spanish Root liquorice that had been sucked too long.

He liked canes that had handles to them. He often used them as a swagger stick, as though still in the army. So we had to try and choose the best quality canes for him. This wasn't difficult, because the shopkeeper always asked who the canes were for, because he knew each teacher's preference. Mr W didn't like his canes to be too thick; they had to be bendy when he waved them up and down, making a suitable 'whooshing' noise. This was part of the limbering up exercise he did when caning one of us. He would usually give us the cane on our behinds. Bending over a desk, he would lift our jacket, the whooshing would begin and then whack! The whooshing wouldn't *always* last a long time, but other times it did. So we were never quite sure when the final blow would fall.

For severe indiscretions, and this applied to that B lad who pinched my marbles, he caned our fingers. He was quite good at this and he must have been sent for to cane children from other classes because his skills were recognised throughout the school, especially by the female members of staff who did not like to cane their children. His skill was such that I could believe that he even gave lessons to the other teachers. One of our hands (he sometimes caned both) would be grasped, palm up and fingers bent backwards and downwards, so that the blow would be a glancing one and sting rather than bruise

It might sound brutal, but we didn't mind at all. It was part of the contract we had with our teachers. They set the rules and we knew what to expect if we broke them. Simple! The stinging was nothing compared to the embarrassment of being found guilty, punished and then having to tell your parents when you got home, because you then had another row.

Although I may be painting a picture of someone who was to be feared, this was only the case if you misbehaved. Most of us liked him, very much, because we got things done with him. We made progress, he gave us discipline and structure and a behaviour pattern which was very helpful. That's the constant dilemma for teachers and leaders; if they are too soft they get little done but everyone feels pleasantly comfortable; if leaders are too harsh they risk suppressing initiative. I think Mr W got it about right. We knew exactly where we stood with him and precisely what the limits were.

It was in his class that we witnessed one of the first full eclipses of the sun. One afternoon, when the eclipse was forecast, the whole school collected in the playground and watched as the world grew darker and darker. We heard birds singing their evening songs as they were fooled into believing the evening had come. The actual eclipse was quite spectacular. Once over, the birds in the park began their dawn chorus, probably feeling quite confused.

The next class, year three, was that of Miss P. She was small, round, wore expensive tweed suits, thick, powder-reinforced makeup, blood red lipstick and pints of heavy perfume. She was also keen on jangly jewellery in the form of necklaces and multiple bracelets.

All this ironmongery made a noise when she wrote on the blackboard, the top of which she could barely reach, meaning she had to stand on tip toe and extend her writing arm to the maximum. The effect on her jangly jewellery and her tweed sleeves was that they worked themselves down her arm and threatened to end up in her armpits. The noise of jewellery clashing was then repeated as it made its way back down to her wrists as she shook her arms free of her suit sleeves. The day was one of constant clanking and, after lunch, yet more perfume filled the air. It seems she took on board more perfume after lunch, aiming for a full tank at all times.

The positive side of this addiction to applied auditory and olfactory effects was that her approaching steps were easy to hear. Being small and rotund, she took small steps and walked quickly, almost like a rapid shuffle. It was rare that she was able to catch us misbehaving when she was not in the classroom. Her approach would be announced by her strident walk and jangling bangles because she always swung her arms when she walked. You could also tell where she'd been: just follow her perfume.

She not only liked perfume from a bottle; she also liked perfume in the form of flowers. Each spring, her south-facing window ledges would be full of hyacinths, especially the one near her desk. She sat on the left of the class under that be-flowered window at a desk which was more modern than Mr W's Dickensian one.

Miss P was keen on nature and it is to her I owe my own interest, sparked at that time in her classroom. She first showed us how 'sticky buds' open out in the spring and the room, not a very large one, was covered with posters (from Shell/BP) of flowers, birds and animals. Even now I still look for the first sticky buds and bring one indoors to open out as my own herald of spring.

She used to encourage us to go into the countryside to collect things and bring them to school. My family were very lucky as we had a car, which meant that I could bring things to school that others didn't have access to.

I remember the family went for a trip one weekend to Tintern Abbey and we parked alongside the River Usk, upstream of it. In the woods behind the car were lots of exotic fungi: red-caps, strange spotted things and all sorts of weird and probably poisonous tree fungi. All these were taken into school in a shoe box.

I became very enthusiastic about this and began to read books on nature study. My grandfather was also keen on this sort of thing, especially on birds, which he sometimes used to trap in nets and keep in cages – illegal now. When he retired he had two canaries which he was teaching to sing. So birds and bird-watching was a particular interest of mine, supported by my grandfather's encouragement and knowledge. But one day in school, my enthusiasm overflowed and got me into real, and rather embarrassing, trouble.

A supply teacher was taking our class and I suppose she was rather stuck for things to do with us. I remember her asking us if any of us had hobbies. Lots of hands went up and the usual things were offered: collecting stamps (I did that); collecting marbles (I had lots of those); riding my bike (I did that too). So my hand was spotted and I said I like bird-watching and nature study. She asked if I could recognise birds and their song and I foolishly suggested that not only did I know my birds, I could even imitate their calls.

So stupid me was asked to stand in front of the class and give a demonstration! How embarrassing! 'This is an owl: *te-wit te-woo*'I said. 'And this one is a Yellow Hammer: *a little bit of bread and no cheese*' (I got this from one of my I Spy Birds books). And that was the extent of my expertise! I think the amusement of the class and the teacher was such that no further work needed to be found that day. I must have glowed as red as a tomato and it taught me not to be so damnably enthusiastic.

Miss P's class was notable for arithmetic. She was in charge of teaching us commercial arithmetic, in pounds, shillings and pence and sorting out our grammar. Both of these I liked. One day, she was away and our class was stuffed in with another class, separated by a half-open wooden partition. The same teacher was teaching two classes in different subjects, all eighty-something of us (our class was forty-seven in number I distinctly remember), and we had an offer from the teacher: do all our sums correctly and we could have a special job.

Always keen to excel I managed the task first and was sent to see the headmistress, Miss H. She seemed to be an old, severe person, who wore lots of powder and makeup but was rarely seen. Like the Queen, she only appeared on special occasions. What she did all day we never knew, but she was obviously a member of the educational aristocracy because even the teachers paid respect to her. Her dress specialism was brown tweed. I cannot remember an occasion when she wore anything else. She had an office at the far end of the corridor, round a bend and next to the staff room. Few pupils entered there.

I was both curious as to what my reward might be and anxious that I was penetrating the head teacher's *sanctum sanctorum*.

The reward was to tutor a new pupil from South Africa in arithmetic and English. He had arrived that day and his English was not good, speaking as he did Afrikaans. His father had been a farmer but had returned to the UK so the lad, whose name I've now forgotten, had to be brought up to speed. Little clever-clogs me got the job.

It was actually very interesting, as well as giving me time off from normal classes, because I could learn as much about his previous life and country as I taught him of ours. These special periods of private tuition lasted for several weeks and we became close friends. But he didn't stay long for some reason and by the end of the school year he had left.

One comment he made on the very first day of working together was how large the classes were. He had attended a private school in South Africa in which the classes were around twenty boys; it was not a mixed gender school either. Our class numbered forty-seven, but that is half the number for which the classrooms in the school had been designed. Not only the architect's plans, but also correspondence and calculations by the founders of the school, show classes sized from sixty to ninety. One classroom in the infants' school was planned for 120 children.

The second and by far the most embarrassing moment in my whole school life also occurred in Miss P's class; but before I tell it, I must also relate the story of how I pretended to blow up the school.

* * *

I have to admit that my imagination has always been a strong point – or some may say my weakest point. One day in the playground, a friend of mine, Brian, who wore the finest hobnail boots I'd seen and had the most fantastically creaky leather jacket, which I always envied, suggested that school was a real pain and wished we didn't have to come each day. Wouldn't it be nice if we could have permanent holidays? Another friend, Robert, suggested the only way to have permanent holidays would be to get rid of the school – perhaps with a bomb.

'I know how bombs work,' I inserted – and I did! But they suggested that rather than talk about it I should make one to show them. This was a challenge. So I set to at home assembling pairs of cotton reels, wrapped in oiled paper and tied with string to look like sticks of dynamite; added some wires and led them off to a battery via an old alarm clock and put the whole thing into a tin – which once held Jacobs Cream Crackers.

I took the thing into school and put it carefully into my desk, showing them that I'd done it! We kept looking knowingly at each other during lessons; me worried that the silly thing would not get the approval I wanted and they worried that they were going to die in the middle of dictation.

At the first break I showed them what I'd made. Robert was fully taken in! He backed away quietly and began telling everyone he saw.

Oh no, I thought, don't go spilling the beans; it's only a pretend bomb!

But he continued to create waves of fear amongst the girls and excitement amongst the boys right across the playground; and my silly tin became the focus of attention for the whole school.

Brian, however, was street-wise and savvy; he saw that the thing was just a mock-up. He laughed and we wondered what on earth we were going to do next.

'I know,' he said, 'let's tell everyone that we'll (notice the 'we') bring the bomb on Friday and set it to go off during the weekend!'

Reluctantly, for by now I realised that this was going to be another 'Yellow Hammer' moment, I agreed. At least I now had a fellow conspirator with me.

So that's what I did: I placed the tin in my desk, after winding up the alarm clock and setting the timer. I thought I would be discovered any moment, because the alarm clock, being an old one, made a clearly audible 'tick-tock' even though it was in the tin. And then we went home.

All weekend I can remember being both anxious (what on earth would Miss H say?) and amused. After all it was only a pretend bomb. But the school was now waiting; all over Grangetown kids were expecting to hear a huge explosion. David U, who lived in the house right next to the primary school, thought it was not at all funny: his whole family might be obliterated.

Were parents questioning their kids at this very moment? Would a delegation arrive at our front door to protest about this wanton destruction of life and property? Would this get into the papers? And I knew all along that this was going to be a real let down on Monday morning.

The weekend passed and Monday came as usual. No explosion.

'I think I set the timer wrong,' I suggested, to a group of disappointed children. Brian came to my aid: 'It was a pretty dangerous thing to do anyway; I've been panicking all weekend – we'd better get rid of it.' So he offered to throw it into the river, which he did. So ended my bomb-making career.

*　*　*

But back to the most embarrassing moment of all in Miss P's class.

I'd been feeling ill that morning and when I went home for lunch I asked my mother to be let off school that afternoon. She thought that I was getting to be too soft and should tough it out. So back to school I went, after listening to the Goon Show on the wireless because it was a Thursday.

That afternoon, for a reason I can't remember, Miss H took our class instead of Miss P. She sat on the lid of the desk right in front of me with her feet on the seat, brown tweeds covering her as usual. And then, all of a sudden, it happened: I was violently sick. My lunch sprayed out on to her lap, all over the desks and the floor. As I hurriedly left the room for the toilets, I remember her asking me rather limply and in some shock: 'So you weren't feeling very well, were you?' I was sick again all the way down the corridor (our classroom was at the end furthest from the cloakrooms) and I was sick for what seemed like hours in the cloakroom too. Poor David U, whom I had almost blown up with my 'bomb', was asked to stay with me.

One of the embarrassing things about this was that we didn't have inside toilets, so I was being sick into a wash hand basin. Poor caretaker! I remember hobbling home through Grange Gardens, having thrown my sick-filled handkerchief into a bin, and told my mother that never again would I go to school if I felt ill. I stayed home the next day and when I returned, everyone seemed much more interested in what I'd done to the headmistress than how I might be feeling.

But the effect on Miss H and her tweed suit awarded me an achievement that few of my peers could better: she never sat near me again.

*　*　*

Our final year in primary school was spent under the august presence of Mr S. He was the teacher who prepared us for the eleven-plus exam and was the most respected of all. He had the classroom directly opposite the stairs as we came up to the first floor (the ground floor being part of the girls' secondary modern school) and was therefore at the opposite end of the school from Miss P. He, as a person, was also her very opposite.

He was a waistcoat-wearing smoker, of uncertain but advanced age, with extremely thin, straight grey hair and lots of facial warts; he was her antithesis. Standing at the head of the line-up in the playground, he would always place his hands on the first child's shoulders and often place the unfortunate child's head and nose directly in line with the waistcoat pocket within which he had just placed a half-smoked fag. He didn't wear perfume either, or gold bangles.

He had a voice which was rather gruff; one which told you not to muck about. But he was kind, especially to those who wanted to work. He had prepared pupils for the eleven-plus exam for decades and was reckoned to be something of a genius at it. He had scanned the exam papers for years back and identified trends, and the probability of certain types of questions occurring and so on; so we felt we were being led by a winner.

The classroom, as I have said, was at one end of the corridor, on the playground side. It was very high-ceilinged and had a large fireplace on the right (as we looked at the blackboard). This was the other side of Mr W's fireplace in fact, so our progress through the school had been somewhat circular. In the winter, the fire was sometimes lit when the central heating broke down and then it was a joy to be near. It was also used to thaw out the milk that would be frozen in winter.

Our desks were old ones. They had a fixed, hard wooden plank for a seat and a rather coarse-grained, slightly sloping top which carried an indent for pens and of course a hole for the inkwell. The two halves, the desk and the seat, were linked together with an ornate cast iron frame. Being of oak and cast iron they didn't move easily which was just as well because Mr S did not like desks being out of line.

A modern-day view of the end of the building. The upper floor window to the right marks the location of Mr S's class.

He, like Mr W, had both a low, modern desk and a high Dickensian one, complete with high stool. He hardly ever sat at it, using it instead for storing the register and various items of stationery, including a bottle of Gloy glue: a white, liquid glue with the consistency of wallpaper paste that came in a pyramid-shaped bottle, which all schools seemed to use. The screw top of the bottle incorporated a wooden handle with a brush for spreading the stuff.

I've not come across Gloy for ages, but it was a superb name and a pleasure to use.

The location of the register on Mr S's high desk was of course known to us and it led to a prank which backfired on us spectacularly. When he was out of the class before registration one day, one of us retrieved the register as usual (covered in brown paper to protect the precious document) and placed it open on his modern desk from where we knew he would take registration. Like all the teachers, he was meticulous about the appearance of this register and the perfect angle at which he drew each 'present' or 'absent' mark, a pattern that was repeated throughout it, making it a work of art.

So imagine his shock and anger when he returned to find the register ready for him but in the centre of it was what appeared to be a large, black ink blot. Without bothering to investigate the blot he flew into a rage which we had never before witnessed and which was so violent it frightened us.

He shouted for the perpetrator to come forward, but this time we were so scared no one moved. We all knew what the next move would be: to pick up his cane. Still no one moved, so he began caning us all. I was near the front (and the nice fire) and was one of the first to get it. Eventually, someone owned up and told him it was only a joke ink blob, something we had bought in a joke shop.

But once a teacher has got himself so worked up that we thought we should ring for an ambulance, and has begun a mass caning of the entire class, it's not a simple matter for him to break out into a smile and a snigger and become all coy! And Mr S experienced just this difficulty. But the caning stopped; and finally, shouting at the perpetrator, who had the final cane, told us all in no uncertain terms that next time this happened our punishment would be worse.

Here our imaginations failed us. We couldn't imagine anything worse than what had just happened. Bottoms, including mine, were throbbing and stinging all over the class; some of the girls were crying, and – well, it was only a joke! But we were now very well aware of how precious that register was to him and we took great care not to even *think* of playing a joke on him that may involve the thing.

One aspect which distinguished Mr S's classroom from all others, was that it had two wheeled blackboards. They were tall boards, supported on wheeled frames, and pivoted on a central pin so that they could be turned completely over. The first time I saw these, I deduced that this class must be for serious work and I was excited by the prospect.

He used these boards extensively and worked hard for us. With a class size of forty-seven, this was tough. The school year was geared towards the eleven-plus exam. As the end of the calendar year approached, so did the exam, which was in February. And so, right from the start of the autumn term, we began rehearsing our answers, doing old papers and using what is still one of my favourite books of all time, *The First Aid in English* (shown left).

This book has within it all one needs to know about grammar: clause analysis, punctuation, similes and metaphors, collective nouns, you name it, the book covers it. It was the best tool we could have had for preparing us for secondary school and is still in print today. The one shown is my 'New' First Aid.

Dictation, mental arithmetic, spelling, arithmetic functions, grammar and clause analysis - we covered them all and with increasing confidence. He particularly wanted us to get our grammar and spelling in order. To this day, one of the words he got us to learn by heart was 'unnecessary' and I still recite it when I need to spell it.

Many of these exercises were done aloud. One of us would suddenly be picked to spell a word, or to do a double-figure multiplication in our head which he would time with his pocket watch (yes, his other waistcoat pocket contained his pocket watch). He insisted that we learn our multiplication tables up to and including thirteen (backwards and well as forwards); that we learn poetry by heart; that we read as much as we possibly could and remember any phrases that struck us as particularly useful in a composition.

This was excellent preparation which stood us all in good stead for the future. I remember incorporating the phrase 'with gay abandon' into an essay on telegram boys during the actual exam.

I can still remember walking through Grange Gardens on the morning of the exam. I was feeling rather anxious. This was, after all, an important, even life-changing, day. Mr W's room was used as the exam room and at nine o'clock the papers were handed out. We were told not to open the paper until instructed to do so, but my enthusiasm got the better of me and I was scolded for doing just that.

It seemed as though all the coaching we'd received was paying off. The arithmetic section contained just the sort of questions we had been rehearsing and the English section contained the clause analysis that I always enjoyed so much. So I began to relax.

Perhaps it was the essay on telegram boys that caused me most effort. The very grand, main post office for Cardiff was then in Westgate Street, from where telegrams could be sent all over the world. So I spent quite some time, I remember, describing it (including its impressive chandeliers) and what I imagined went on in the back rooms where the boys would pick up telegrams and depart on their bicycles to deliver messages, joyful or sad, all over Cardiff. I managed to insert the phrase I had memorised into this description, imagining what it would be like to be one of the boys, peddling as fast as he could (with gay abandon, in fact!) down Westgate Street.

But what was the future to hold for us? Once the exam was over, we waited with bated breath for the outcome, an outcome that both shocked and pleased me.

On the day the results were delivered to the school, the headmistress came to the classroom (a rare and royal occasion) to announce the results in tangible terms. What I mean by this is that the whole classroom was physically re-arranged (the very first time desks were moved), so the desks were pushed to each side of the room, leaving a central gap in the middle. Down this gap, several low benches were laid end-to-end, forming a barrier or dividing line.

Then Mr S started calling out names. As he did so, against each name was attached an instruction: "Go to the left (or right) and sit at a desk." It quickly became apparent that those told to sit at the left-hand desks had failed the exam and those on the right had passed. I waited and waited, because Noyes is half way through the alphabet, and finally I had a seat, on the right. I had passed! But who else was sitting there? Not many. I wouldn't like to give a figure all these years later, but I think approximately a quarter of us passed out of forty-seven.

Needless to say, the desks on the 'failed' side could barely accommodate all the failures so that we who sat in the relatively empty 'passed' desks felt both elated and sad. The emptiness of the seats matched the emptiness we felt. The rest of our friends were not coming with us, including my partners involved in the bomb plot and the ink joke.

Returning home with the news that I was going to a grammar school sent my mother into orbit. She had been brought up in a large, very poor family that on several occasions had been living on the streets, and she'd had to struggle hard to get into grammar school in Durham. She had a burning desire, therefore, for both my brother and me to do the same and was very supportive throughout our schooling. She realised full well what a good education was worth and what it had cost her.

My father too was happy. Having left school at fifteen, he didn't know what lay ahead of me and what a grammar school education meant. But it was a happy time, and I received a new bicycle from my grandparents as a reward, which was just about the perfect gift for someone of my age. It was a bike that I treasured for years until going to university.

In those days, a relatively small proportion of children went to grammar schools; and of those, only a smaller proportion sat and passed A-levels and went to university. I think the overall figure for university entrants was only about 3-5%.

Many would argue that this was a socially divisive and perhaps a cruel selection method. But I have to say that once the dust had settled and we all went our various ways, it actually showed itself to have sorted out very effectively those who were interested in academic work and those who were interested in gaining a trade or craft. Additionally, and importantly, if a mistake was identified within the first year of attending a secondary modern school, pupils were moved to a grammar school anyway, so a safety net did operate. A few of these children did join us in our grammar school class.

In spite of what some politicians say, grammar schools promoted social mobility. If children, like me, from working class backgrounds, had been in a comprehensive school in Grangetown filled with children from the same area, we probably would have stayed in that same social class.

There is of course nothing wrong with that, but we would not have encountered the children of solicitors, company directors, doctors, academics and engineers. To have stayed where we had been brought up, in a school in which the majority of parents like mine, had unskilled jobs and little education, would have limited our horizons; by attending a grammar school we realised from the jobs and careers our peers' fathers had, that there were career possibilities we had never imagined.

These incidental observations of our peers' parents' lives nurtured ambitions we wouldn't otherwise have had. My brother and I (and all our friends who went to grammar schools from Grangetown) are examples of this.

If one adds to this the fact that secondary modern schools had excellent arrangements with fine technical colleges and apprenticeship schemes, the system seemed to produce the skills we needed and identified in a pragmatic way the practical and academic choices of the children involved. The value of a technical education with apprenticeships is only now being recognised once more.

I won't write about my time in grammar school except to say that I know I had one of the best educations I can imagine. It was a fine, ambitious school, proud of its achievements, which challenged us in all sorts of ways, setting high standards of achievement and behaviour. It's an education for which I shall always be grateful. We had gown-wearing masters and mistresses, proud uniforms and house badges, formal assemblies and a huge eisteddfod every year. It also had its own orchestra and choir and we put on at least one major public concert and a play each year.

It therefore saddens me when I drive past Cathays High School now to see its physical decay and hear about its rowdy and ill-disciplined children. I think the government that scrapped grammar schools was trying to tackle the wrong thing. There was nothing wrong, and everything right, about grammar schools; the real problem was the lack of support for secondary modern schools.

As a personal addendum, my father also attended the Board School and I have a photograph of him with his classmates in what would have been the equivalent of Miss P's class.

My father, second from the right in the first row standing (next to the very tall lad wearing a cap)

CHAPTER SIX

Going Places

Clarence Road Bridge - September 1937

Trams

Trams were exciting things to ride on, but very noisy. The noise came not only from their metal wheels riding on metal rails, but also from the glass rattling in the wooden window frames. I used to wonder why they didn't crack.

The glass panes were simply held in place by strips of varnished wood held down by brass screws. This may seem an odd detail to remember, but the screws on the bottom part of the window were at eye level for a small child and they were worn smooth and shiny by the hands and elbows of many passengers. It was their shininess that I noticed.

The vehicles could give passengers a rough ride when rounding curves, because the axles were fixed, so that their wheels had to sashay around the curve. This resulted in a side-to-side motion that could be quite severe if doing so at speed.

Trams were wooden vehicles. Wood was everywhere, except in the driver's cab in the front. The seats were wooden and slatted, on both their seats and backs and were rather hard and uncomfortable. The exterior of the vehicle was wood fixed to a metal frame. The floors were made of wood slats with gaps between them that ran lengthwise down the tram and could be a little dangerous when wet. Women's shoes with a small heel could get stuck in gaps or simply just go from under them on the slippery boards. I often wondered why the slats were not fixed laterally so as to avoid the problem. (I was always destined to be an engineer.)

Trams were very narrow vehicles. This enabled them to run in the middle of the road, whilst other traffic used the rest of it. Their narrowness meant that it was also quite a crush inside.

Their ceilings were arched. Panels, painted white, between wooden beading made a rather pleasant inside to them, but bearing in mind that nearly everyone smoked at that time and not only cigarettes, the ceilings upstairs (the designated smoking area) quickly took on a brown colour. In the winter, when people with wet clothing got onto the tram, the tobacco tars on the ceilings would begin to dissolve in the water vapour and run down the curved panels in streaks. You needn't look hard to see if the tram was old or new; just look up at the ceiling.

Running the length of the tram, in the centre of the ceiling, was a thin red rope or cord, running between brass eyes. When pulled by the conductor, it would ring a bell in the driver's cab and he would stop at the next stop.

Conductors walked up and down the tram handing out pre-printed tickets. There was no need to buy one before boarding. If they wanted to annoy you, they sometimes gave your change in pennies, so it was always best to make sure you either had the right change or at least nothing of a large denomination, which would be greeted with suitable mumbling and grumbling as he fished in his capacious and often heavy, black leather bag for change.

Cardiff bus ticket

Standing right down the front was my favourite position, which was allowed only if all the seats were occupied. From this position, one could watch the driver at work. He had no seat and his main pre-occupation besides looking out for people or other vehicles was regulating the speed and applying the brakes. The rest took care of itself, being on rails.

The brakes were simple oak blocks which rubbed on the wheels to slow the tram down; but the speed regulator was interesting. It was a black cast iron column on the top of which was a brass handle. As he wound this one way or the other, the speed would pick up or slow down.

Getting upstairs was difficult. It was accessed via steep, narrow and twisting steps. In fact, it was so difficult to climb upstairs, and to descend them, that only men were encouraged to go up there. Smoking was also only allowed upstairs, so it was more-or-less a men only area.

Being on a railway system separate from other road users, meant that trams could keep good time. One could set a watch to them. But they had their dangers: being in the centre of the road, passengers had to board them by crossing the lanes used by other vehicles, including horse-drawn ones and bicycles. But the conductor was on hand to stop other traffic because the trams had priority. He would also ensure that passengers were aided with their bags and luggage and did not allow the tram to move off until everyone was seated.

No.21 tram to Cathays, in Century of Trams Exhibition, Birmingham

Folding pushchairs or even small fixed ones hadn't been invented then; all prams were large-wheeled ones and capacious. It would have been impossible to take them onto a tram; there was just no room and the effort needed to lift them would need two people anyway.

Mothers wishing to take their babies to town on a tram would carry them in their arms, usually in a shawl wrapped around the body for support. Mothers walked miles with them in that position and carried their shopping back too, although most of the weekly food shopping was done in local shops and most had delivery boys who brought them to the house on a bicycle with a capacious front carrier for the purpose.

Delivery bicycle

Trolleybuses

Then, along came a new and far more comfortable form of transport: the trolleybus. It looked like a double-decker bus but with a totally flat front and was electrically driven, like the trams. Its comfortable seats and modern glass windows (retained in place by proper rubber seals) meant it was also much quieter than the tram - outside as well as in. So much so that pedestrians and cyclists sometimes didn't hear them. They were fitted with much more powerful motors so that their acceleration, even when full, was impressive.

They were very comfortable and smooth running. The seats were upholstered rather than being of wooden slats and they were wider than trams, allowing more passengers, although prams were still not accommodated until later when folding pushchairs came along. These and any luggage was stored by the conductor beneath the stairs.

Trolleybus routes covered the whole of the city. Unlike trams, they took their place amongst ordinary traffic; there was no special track or lane for them. Having rubber wheels, the electricity couldn't pass to earth via steel rails like trams so that they had to be powered by two overhead wires, positive and negative. They did not always enjoy an easy co-habitation with other vehicles.

No.6 Pier Head trolley bus

At junctions, where pairs of overhead wires had to cross in complex points arrangements, the overhead current collectors on the vehicles sometimes came off the wires. When this happened, the conductor had to get out, pull a very long bamboo pole, about 30 feet long from beneath the vehicle and using the hook on the end of it, try and coax the spring-loaded current-

79

collecting arms back onto the electric wires. If a trolleybus was really stuck, due perhaps to a power failure of the system, it did have a battery that could move it out of the way of traffic.

Reattaching the collector arms may not seem complicated, but when one realises that this bamboo pole was so long (taller than the trolleybus) that vehicles behind the trolleybus often had to be coaxed into reversing to allow it to be withdrawn, one can imagine the chaos that resulted at busy times and at busy junctions. There was many a scene of chaos as trolleybuses held up traffic whilst the hapless conductor struggled with the collector arms. His main problem was that the springs pushing up against the overhead wires were quite strong and he had to overcome them.

All travellers on trolleybuses will tell you how sometimes, when first setting off from a stop, the driver may try to accelerate too quickly and a cut-out would operate in the cab, breaking the current. The vehicle would come to a sudden halt and would have to be re-set. Sometimes this could result in people being thrown around, so conductors had to make sure that frail and vulnerable passengers were seated and safe before pressing the bell, twice to start and once for a stop. Modern vehicles, with no conductors, have no one to watch over passengers like this and certainly no one to help them with shopping or prams.

Buses

Diesel engines were not used in buses, their engines being petrol ones. They were mostly single-decker vehicles and were remnants of the old *char-à-bancs*. They were simple vehicles, constructed like old stage coaches, using a wooden frame mounted on a chassis. The wooden frame was covered with wooden panels and the roof on the oldest buses was often of canvas stiffened with paint. They also had wooden slatted seats and wood panelled ceilings and floors.

The overall shape of them may appear a little curious now, probably because they had elements in them that harked back to the shape of stage coaches. The roof was often curved; the back was rounded, in fact little in those days seemed to have a straight line. Curves were in. It was the 1960s that saw straight lines become the vogue, in furniture, architecture and even fashion.

The driver sat in what was a small glass box, on the right of course, and on his left was the bonnet of the engine at a lower level and outside the vehicle. So his cab had glass on all sides: the windscreen, the door and the (sliding) window over the engine. Behind him was a fixed glass window connected with the main body of the bus, which was often covered by a blind. The cab occupied one half of the width of the vehicle and the engine the other half: they were side by side.

Straddling them was a large chrome radiator, sometimes with a circular temperature gauge mounted on the top in the case of the oldest buses. The gauge was visible to passengers near the front, and it would be watched with great interest when the bus was climbing hills. It was not unusual on a summer's day for the gauge needle to swing over to 'hot' and the engine boil over so that the bus was forced to stop. A large can of water was always carried on board to top up the water cooling system, once it had cooled down.

Single-decker town bus

The driver was effectively isolated, there being no connection between the driver and passengers on this design of bus. For excursions, which used buses that were hired for carrying private groups, a more open arrangement between the driver and passengers gradually changed, developing into the style we are now used to, where the driver and passengers share the same overall space.

Bus companies offered mystery tours on their single-decker buses, the passengers paying their fare but having no idea where they would be taken. Usually, they took townsfolk into the countryside, which is where the buses encountered hills. So besides the destination being a mystery, the ability of the vehicle to arrive there was also a mystery and added to the thrill and excitement of a day out. Such tours were very popular with urban dwellers, many of whom did not normally get to enjoy fresh air.

Much smoke was in the atmosphere, especially during the winter when every house had a coal fire or two. One can imagine the amount of smoke that came from a street of, say, a hundred houses, all burning soft bituminous, sulphurous coal. That image then has to be multiplied by street after street.

Adjacent industry also contributed to the general fug, of course, and in winter there were often very dense fogs. I can vividly remember waiting at a bus stop unable to see across the street, a distance of about thirty feet.

During such fog, or smog, we would not only hear cars and lorries sounding their horns to make themselves known to other road users, we could also hear the doleful moan of fog horns at the docks, guiding ships into port. The headlights on vehicles were no more than a faint, yellow glow and many accidents occurred during winter fogs.

As for the health hazard of dense smog, it is difficult to say what the effects were, in that many men had poor lungs anyway due to smoking and due to their work; life expectancy was much lower than it is now. In fact, in the 1950s, a man who retired at sixty-five could not expect to reach his seventieth birthday, the average post-retirement period being just three years.

Petrol engines at this time, besides being low powered, were very unreliable and inefficient. This meant that the gearing on them had to be very low. When they started off or tried climbing a hill, the high-pitched whine of the gearbox was a unique sound which I can still remember. It gave one the impression that the gearbox was in pain, as though completely dry of oil and its parts were having difficulty dealing with each other. A scream is the nearest sound I can match to it.

Tangible proof of the suffering of these gearboxes was to feel how hot they became, which was easy to do because they projected into the passenger space, often covered by a large chrome cover with the maker's name on them, such as Dennis. This cover was always hot and on a summer's day it was not the most welcome feature of the interior. Sitting up front was not a favourite position unless one

Double-decker town bus

had to. Sitting in the back was not nice either, because of the exhaust fumes. If anyone was going to be sick, they were usually sitting in the back, being quietly poisoned.

Possibly not more than about 60% of the petrol was properly burned, some of it infiltrating the interior of the car from poor gasket joints within the exhaust system. Such joints were simply made of thin cardboard with a bit of sticky red-lead added to make a seal. It was not unusual for exhaust smoke to be seen coming from beneath the dashboard of a car or from beneath the feet of its driver.

To drive a petrol-driven bus required stamina and skill. It was not possible to simply move the gear lever from one gear to another as now; there was no synchromesh. So a driver (and this applied to cars too) had to depress the clutch, increase or decrease the speed of the engine, listen to the whine of the engine and gearbox, depress the clutch again when the driver had guessed the speed was just about right and try to push the gear lever into a new gear. Bearing in mind that no part of the steering or the gear change was power-assisted, this meant that the gear lever had to be very long (for leverage) and the driver strong. Drivers often wore gloves to ease the wear on their hands due to such manoeuvres.

It was common for drivers of all vehicles to miss gear changes and this meant that the car or bus would slow down. Then the driver would have to engage an even lower gear, especially if the vehicle were climbing a hill. This in turn meant that the vehicle would lurch forward when the lower gear was eventually found; the lurching and jolting being a feature of the ride, accompanied by the grinding of the gear box and the continuous moan of the back axle

Similarly, the steering wheel was, compared with today's, of huge diameter and, because complex steering linkages were not then made, it was almost horizontal. So drivers effectively sat at one side of this large wheel, which was about at stomach level, and had to drive by pushing and pulling either side of it. This too was demanding.

The brakes were very crude; they were un-aerated blocks which often overheated and sometimes burst into flame if applied too consistently when going down a steep hill. I can remember my father in our old Ford Prefect car, and the Austin 7 that preceded it, panicking on many a hill which now we might not even recognise as a hill.

An example of a single-decker bus with a shared driver and passenger space is shown above. For a fully laden *char-à-banc* bowling down a hill, the driver had to anticipate very carefully what had to be done to slow the vehicle down; he had to select early the lowest gear he could find and only use the brakes when necessary. There were even signs on the steepest hills (which coach drivers knew about anyway) advising which gears they should be in at any one time to avoid a calamity. My father often had to apply both the handbrake and footbrake to help slow down the car in such circumstances. Brakes were very poor.

Because vehicles, like everything else at that time, were constructed from organic materials – wood, horse hair, cloth and varnish – they had a smell which was quite different to modern vehicles. Organic materials absorb smells. In cars, the ceilings were covered in a felt cloth, the leather seats were stuffed with horse hair and all these absorbent materials picked up the smell of leaking petrol from the engine and the smell of the exhaust, which contained large quantities of unburned petrol. Not to mention the smell of pipes and cigarettes (many men smoked pipes) which gave buses, especially, a smell all their own. Entering each vehicle was to experience a set of smells unique to it, but always with the common denominators of petrol and old and usually very dusty moquette seat covers.

Charabanc

Passengers in buses knew that their driver worked hard in his tiny cab. They would often break out into song as though to urge him on. Such singing was inevitable. On the way out, songs such as *She'll be coming round the mountain when she comes*, *I've got a lovely bunch of coconuts* or *ten green bottles* would suffice; but on the way back it had to be something like a solo from someone, or songs such as *Show Me the Way to Go Home* or *Sweet Molly Malone*. All great fun. It was surprising how often there appeared a comedian amongst the passengers who told jokes or perhaps played a harmonica which he carried in his top pocket.

Whatever the source of amusement, outings in such vehicles were always memorable.

Cars

In the 1940s and 50s, cars were small and very expensive. Steel and other materials were scarce and the UK was just about the only car manufacturer left in Europe. In order to earn foreign currency, most car production was aimed at export markets, so that prospective UK owners often had to wait a long time to get a new one. Consequently, the second-hand car market was inflated and all cars were very expensive.

This quasi-monopoly ought to have been seized on as a huge opportunity for the UK to invest, to innovate and thus to grow huge potential export markets; but it was not to be so. Perhaps the country was just too tired, or the manufacturers were too lazy; whatever the reason, our car industry closed its eyes to the needs of overseas customers and kept churning out the same designs with almost the same layout.

By this I mean that although cars for export to the continent were left-hand drive, little was done except the bare minimum, to adapt cars for the different driving conditions. Of course the steering wheel and pedals were swopped to the left of the car, but not all the gauges were moved over. They also refused to change the side of the car on which it could be locked. In the UK, the driver's door is on the right and so is the car's door lock. Many cars for export continued to have the door lock on the right even though the driver was getting in and out on the left.

As if the arrogant omission of such modifications for foreign customers was not enough, they had little choice as to colour. If a black car was the next off the production line, then that's what the customer had. It's no wonder that with the Allies investing huge amounts in resurrecting the German and French auto industries, the UK gradually lost its markets, its customers and its reputation. A similar phenomenon occurred in the motorcycle industry, where the UK's bikes were once considered the world's best but little innovation took place. Eventually, the Japanese with their new plants and production methods, swept the board.

Perhaps it is difficult to imagine the emotions of a post-war family owning its first car. I remember vividly how my own family reacted once we could afford one in 1948.

The gasworks had been nationalised, alongside other utilities and my grandfather together with many other shareholder employees, received payment from the government for his shares. This allowed us to have a car, an Austin 7, pictured below.

The realisation suddenly hit us that we could now go anywhere. I remember looking down the length of our street and realising that the tarmac on which I stood was in continuous contact with, say Barry Island, or England, or Scotland – why not? Although the latter would probably be well beyond the stamina of such a small car and its driver. Setting out on a journey in such cars was easy, but there was no guarantee you would get there!

Engines were small and inefficient compared with today's. In fact, the popular but low-powered side-valve engines fitted to the Austin 7 were given the nickname of 'spit and hope' when it came to lubrication. They didn't have oil pumps to lubricate the engine, the moving parts simply splashed in the sump oil with the hope that they would be adequately lubricated. This worked after a fashion if a vehicle was on level ground, but going uphill meant that the sump oil moved to the back of the engine, leaving the moving parts in the front without oil.

Austin Seven

Many efforts were made by both engine manufacturers and fuel companies to improve engine efficiency. One trick was to offer customers at petrol stations a 'shot'. This was not an intravenous injection of some kind of mind-altering drug for the driver, but was a magic additive to the petrol to 'improve upper cylinder performance', something I never understood. Petrol stations were of course manned then, members of the public not being allowed to touch the equipment which pumped out highly flammable petrol. My father often asked for 'two shots and two, please' which meant two shots of this magic stuff and two gallons of petrol.

Other wheezes of a similar nature were tried on motorists, one being the Mobile Economy Run. This was Mobile petrol's attempt to show motorists that their petrol could achieve amazing consumption figures. Someone from the company (I assume) would set out on a journey, often a long one, and by driving extremely carefully would record how many miles per gallon he had achieved. These figures were advertised and updated regularly, and motorists were challenged to do better by using Mobile petrol.

We had many an enjoyable excursion in the Austin 7 and bearing in mind that there were six of us, it was quite a feat fitting in. Eventually, it was realised that my younger brother and I were taking up more and more space and so an upgrade in size was needed. This time we went for a Ford car, the Ford Prefect. It had four doors, which was a great improvement and lots more space; it even had a boot where we kept not only tools for unexpected repairs, but also a Primus Stove.

Ford Prefect

These were wonderful inventions. The stove used paraffin that was pumped upwards through a tiny jet that had previously been heated by burning a doughnut ring of methylated spirits. Once encountering the heated jet, the paraffin would vapourise and produce a very hot blue flame.

Once roaring away, one could cook on them or at least make a cup of tea. Many a family car had one of these in the car boot. Really innovative owners would put the stove into a large biscuit tin, having cut out access panels in the side to be able to pour the methylated spirits into the pre-heater ring and then to pump up the reservoir of paraffin. Having a stove in such a metal tin meant that its flame was protected from the wind. If the flame blew out, hot unlit paraffin fumes would be emitted, which could explode if they then encountered a flame.

The design of the Primus Stove was quite old, having been invented in the 1920s; its basic principle having been used to power blowlamps for plumbers.

* * *

I shall close this chapter with an anecdote which illustrates how car users were often exposed to risk, something we got used to and learned to manage. It concerns trips to the West Country.

There were no bridges over the Severn in those days, so we had to use a ferry, which used to sail between Aust, near the first suspension bridge, and the opposite bank in England. The ferry saved 90 miles of driving to Gloucester and back down the other side of the estuary. So it was worthwhile, bearing in mind that most cars didn't go faster than 45 mph, or 50 mph at the outside.

We used to queue for some time to board the ferry, depending on how many cars wanted to use it. On the Welsh side, when it came to our turn to board, we had to drive our vehicle down a stone ramp and then towards the water. The ferry was a front-loading boat and was moored side-on at right-angles to the ramp. So drivers had to make a right-angled turn at the bottom.

The Severn is tidal, with the world's second-largest tidal flow of 47 feet at Barry, so that when the tide went out, it left slippery mud and seaweed on this stone ramp. Drivers, with usually only three gears, poor steering and brakes that hardly worked, had to take their cars down it and turn sharply at the bottom onto the ferry.

This was not a job for the faint-hearted. Once, with all six of us on board, Dad drove gingerly down and we could feel that although he had engaged a low gear and had partially applied the handbrake, the car was not slowing down as it neared the waiting ferry; it was slipping on seaweed and mud. Applying the breaks harder made it worse and we could see the sea straight ahead of us.

As bad luck would have it, the left front wheel caught on something and slewed the car anticlockwise, the rear wheels sliding

Advertisement for a portable Primus stove

towards the sea. Now the car was sliding down the ramp sideways and we risked passing the ferry! Sheer good luck made the rear wheels hit the ramp of the ferry and Dad managed to stop the car.

With hearts pounding, we all got out, except my grandmother, who was not too good on her feet, and with help from the ferry crew the car was turned enough to board the ferry. Poor Dad! But he managed it. Such incidents were not rare in the history of the ferry; it was a more or less normal occurrence for the crew.

Aust ferry

CHAPTER SEVEN
The Sound of Fire

If I have one lasting impression of where I lived, it is the background noise of industry. Across the River Taff was Curran's Steel works, constantly clanking as scrap steel was picked up by cranes to be dropped, with a loud crash, into the furnace wagons. The furnaces, especially when loaded or unloaded, sent huge flames and smoke into the sky, accompanied by showers of sparks that were spectacular at night.

The roar of the furnaces was continuous and mixed into this background was the sound of steam engines, chuffing and puffing as they shunted wagons at the docks or at Grangetown Station, preparing long trains of them for the various works or returning them to coal mines in the Rhondda Valley.

When the wind was from the north, I could hear the sound of the London express trains whistling as they left the central station in Cardiff. Ships horns blew and fog horns moaned.

To visit the docks, you had to cross the River Taff via a steel swing bridge. Approaching the dock gates, there would often be large numbers of men loitering outside the port's offices offering themselves as stevedores.

Once in the docks themselves, there was a general air of industry and pace: steam engines moved hither and thither; cranes lifted and turned their heads as ships were unloaded. Long trains of coal wagons would be tipped noisily and dustily into the open holds of ships; other cranes would dip their noses into the holds of ships from exotic ports. These carried rare timber, cereals, fruit (especially bananas), vegetables and meat which, once the cranes had lowered them onto the quayside, needed to be handled by hand.

When they were ready to take to sea, ships' boilers would be stoked up and smoke belched out of their funnels, often accompanied by the ship's horn which could make you jump out of your skin if you were near and not expecting it.

* * *

It is perhaps difficult to fully appreciate the shock that the sheer busyness, the noise, the industry and the danger that the docks would give a visitor.

Once inside the dock gates, a young boy would leave behind the relatively calm pace of ordinary life, that of shops, school, parks and bicycles. As soon as he crossed the threshold he would be hit by a strong sense of urgency, almost verging on panic as ships entering the docks had to be turned around as quickly as possible to catch the tide. The reputation of the docks depended on it; customers were waiting for their goods and investors wanted profits.

The largest investment was, of course, in the extraction and export of coal, although in the 19th century the port was also one of the largest iron-exporting ports. Due to a huge investment in mechanisation, the port gained a reputation for turning ships

This painting is by Lionel Walden, an American artist who was impressed by the scale of activity of the Cardiff Docks. It is entitled simply *Cardiff Docks* and was painted in 1894. It is interesting that he has captured both steam ships and sailing ships at this time.

around fast; in fact, it was reckoned that most medium-sized ships could enter the port on the tide and be leaving it on the next, just twelve hours later.

The major investor and, indeed, effectively the creator of Cardiff Docks, was the second Marquess of Bute, who opened his Great West Dock in 1833. At the time, it was one of the largest docks in the world, able to accommodate 160 ships at its miles of quayside. The third Marquess, shown in the photograph, continued to expand the docks so that by the early 20th century almost 7 miles of quayside were available for shipping. When he was born, the third Marquess was said to be the richest baby in the world. He benefited not only from the huge inheritance from his father but also from fresh wealth due to marriage and legacies left him by relatives, such as the Earl of Dumphries.

Since he created vast wealth, it would be easy to assume that he was a harsh, power-hungry man, but this is not the case. He was a polymath of some distinction: a renowned scholar, a generous benefactor to Scottish

2nd Marquis of Bute

Coal Exchange

universities and especially Cardiff, he had a genuine concern for the poor. A religious man, he was also fiercely supportive of Wales and its language, speaking it fluently. Perhaps his principle oddity, if we need to look for one, was his total fascination with all things medieval. This he expressed lavishly in the reconstruction and decoration of both Cardiff Castle and his summer lodge, Castell Coch.

The Marquess invested in railways connecting the docks with sources of coal in the Rhondda Valleys. He also invested in the extraction of the very product, coal, that his port was handling, buying up mineral rights to large tracts of land. As if that were not to provide sufficient riches, he invested in other railways, ship repairing and warehousing.

Perhaps the most significant demonstration of the importance of Cardiff Docks was the establishment of the International Coal Exchange in 1888. On its trading floor, shown above, the price of coal and the price of shipping it was set across the world. A further example of the pride and the riches associated with the Butes' investments is the Pierhead Building, dating from 1894. It may well win the prize for the most expensive and elaborate set of docks' offices anywhere.

Pier Head Building, Cardiff Docks

* * *

When it was foggy, and there were often dense fogs, foghorns would send out their deep, resonant two-note warnings, sounding doleful and lonely. These calls were sometimes answered by ships' horns as they approached their destination. You could therefore tell, just by the background noise, what was going on. And if anyone wanted to see spectacular displays of steam and fire, they had only to walk around to experience them first hand.

Grangetown had its own small railway station, the remnant of which is still there, albeit a crude, minimalist metal structure offering little shelter now. It used to be a lovely spot at which to wait for trains. Built high up on the railway embankment, it gave a fine view of the countryside outside our island and across its rooftops. It had a lovely waiting room, with a coal fire, painted overall in cream and brown, the standard colours of the Great Western Railway.

We had another station available to us, reached by using the swing bridge over the Taff. It enabled us to travel to Caerphilly and the Rhondda Valleys.

Catching a train was something thrilling and special. Waiting for one was particularly exciting. If you leaned over the platform edge you could see quite a way down the line from Grangetown Station towards the central station and spot the train on its way. Looking the other way, towards Penarth, the full length of a train could be seen as it crossed the railway bridge over the River Ely. As it neared the station, the rails would sing, which was the signal that it was close.

No matter how much warning you had of an approaching train, nothing could prepare you for its actual arrival as it passed you. The huge mass of the engine, its heat, noise, steam and smoke, were always a shock. Even when at rest, engines gave off their power. Scorching heat radiated from the sides of the boiler and its firebox, preventing you from getting too near. This was particularly true of the huge express locomotives.

All engines made their own particular noises when at rest like this. Metal contracted and expanded, making clicking noises; steam escaped from small pipes and valves, hot water dripped as steam condensed on various elements such as the main pistons. A slow, rhythmic clanking, like a heartbeat, often emanated from within the engine as its components cooled or heated up. It seemed like a monster sleeping, full of latent power.

Although these branch line engines were interesting, it was every boy's dream to be near a main line express. They were truly magnificent machines, often painted in a beautiful dark green with gold edging outlining their sleek profiles. Brass was polished to a bright shine and you could see your face in the huge steel drive mechanisms.

For a few pennies, we would buy platform tickets for the central station which allowed us to stay there all day if we wished, taking down engine numbers and their proud names and of course getting close to them. Studying how trains were made up, how the guards wagon at the end of a train was loaded with mail and goods; looking into the first class dining car at the meals being served: there was much to see.

We usually took the opportunity to glance into the driver's cab when one of the express trains arrived; either en route to London or stopping briefly on its way to Swansea. London seemed a world away, so that to have contact with the trains that actually went there felt as though we were in touch with a spacecraft, one that visited alien worlds far away. Could this machine really take all these people and all these carriages to such a distant and exciting world capital? Seeing the firebox glowing, brass and steel shining, we thought the men who drove them were superhuman, our heroes.

Perhaps the most impressive sensation was when the platform shook and shuddered beneath our feet as hundreds of tons of engine and carriages drew in. Its huge shining wheels and thrusting cranks and pistons spoke of strength and power. Hearing one of these monsters running across a bridge when you were beneath it was quite frightening in a self-imposed way. If we spotted a train at a station, even a small train at a small station like Grangetown, we would deliberately wait under a bridge for the train to cross it so as to experience the thunder it made.

The same can be said of the noise they made running through Cardiff's Central Station, the whole of which shook under the shuddering weight. The large express trains to London (the so-called 'Pacific' and 'King-class' locomotives) were really huge, pulling their own coal and water tenders and made the loudest noise of all, shaking any station to its foundations. Here was power indeed.

*　*　*

Frightening ourselves was something we indulged in from time to time. One favourite experience was using the subway which ran beneath the River Ely and connected Grangetown with Penarth

Harbour and Docks. It was, of course, a dark, damp and rather eerie place that echoed at each footstep.

Constructed from cast iron ribs, it had spooky acoustics all of its own, the lighting was often deficient or non-existent and water dripped noisily from the walls and roof. It could be quite exciting to penetrate the darkness and reach a point at which, because of the bends in it, we could no longer see either the entrance or the exit; the point at which we were enveloped in total darkness if the lights were out. We were far from rescue, the cold beginning to seep into our bones. The constant drip, drip of water was accompanied by strange echoes as a stranger entered the tunnel behind us. Who's coming? Is it a murderer? How much water is above our heads? Should we turn around now before it gets any darker? What's that noise?

At least, this is what we told our little brothers!

Penarth – Grangetown Subway

* * *

As train travellers, we had the choice of just two classes of carriage: first or third. For some reason of sensitivity, the classification of second class was not used and it became third. Third class often had wooden seats on small branch lines whilst first class had softer ones. We never travelled first class.

Early on, most branch line trains didn't have corridors, just a door on either side of each carriage compartment, and used according to which side the platform was on. This could be dangerous; there were cases of people opening the wrong door and falling out onto the railway line.

The seating was arranged against each side of this narrow rectangular compartment facing each other, the walls decorated with black and white photographs of holiday destinations. Above the seats, were string-woven luggage nets.

Third Class railway carriage

The windows always fascinated me. Firstly, they were fitted with folded leather 'curtains' that could be pulled down over the two fixed windows either side of the door, Roman blind fashion, and a wooden stick at the bottom secured it in various notches depending on how low you wanted the blind to be. The doors had windows, which could be pulled down to open them, and also internal latches that slid across, so that it was not necessary to reach outside to open the door as it is now.

It was the mechanism of the window itself that I was most interested in. The window slid down within the thickness of the door. A thick leather strap, about 2.5 inches wide and about a quarter of an inch thick, was attached at its base, with a number of holes along the centre of it, just like a belt. If you wanted the window fully closed, you pulled up hard on the leather strap, which lifted the window into its top position. It would be secured there by pushing one of the holes in the strap over a small brass button on the wooden door panel. Other positions were possible so as to allow fresh air into the compartment, the window being secured in its intermediate positions in the same way by using the holes in the strap. It was simple, but effective.

The end of the strap was rolled tightly and sewn into a Swiss Roll shape, so that if a passenger, struggling with the (rather heavy) wooden window were to drop the strap, the roll of leather at the end would prevent the window from disappearing completely into the door.

Train speeds, especially on the small branch lines, were low and not much more than 40 or 50 mph. These lovely lines meandered around obstacles and followed rivers and woodland so that they had lots of bends in them. This meant that if you put your head out of the window, a practice much frowned upon, you could see the length of the train snaking along a bend and get a good idea of the overall length of the train. Not only passing trains made this dangerous; there was also a large amount of soot and ash, some of it hot, given off by the stack of the train and these smuts could damage your eyes. But we still did it.

The big enemy of trains, as it still is now, is a gradient. There was one which was always problematic, called The Dingle, which was on the way to Penarth. The train would leave Grangetown Station, curve noisily across a steel bridge over the River Ely (at which point we always looked out for our grandfather's allotment) and turn left towards Penarth at the small station of Cogan and aim for the sea. The route largely followed Penarth Road, so that we could gauge our speed by comparing it to the cars and lorries. The track would pass through a short tunnel before reaching Cogan Station and then cross over the road to Dingle Station.

It then entered a sleepy, tree-covered and largely hidden cutting that was a point at which engines could take on water and raise more steam for the climb up the steep gradient to Penarth. Sometimes, if the driver had not managed to maintain a boiler full of steam, we waited perhaps ten minutes until the engine filled up again. Then came the slow chuff-chuff of the engine as it climbed and laboured under its weight of carriages against the incline. Huge blasts of steam were blown from its pistons as the driver piled on all the pressure he could, to get those hundreds of tons of steel and passengers to move up the hill. The passengers seemed to tense themselves as it laboured: 'will we make it?' we wondered.

Sometimes the wheels of the engine would slip, especially in winter and the driver would release some sand onto the rails to help the wheels grip. Sand was kept in steel boxes on the sides of the engine for this purpose and he could release it slowly from the cab.

Occasionally, an engine would lose traction because the driver applied too much power and then the whole train would slip a little. This was alarming, but not so alarming as not being able to stop at a station. When this happened the engine would come to a final stop some distance from the correct spot on a platform and passengers on the platform would have to run to catch it up. Worse, passengers wanting to get off the train would have no platform on which to step, and could be in real difficulty. In such cases, the guard or station master would guide the train as it backed into its proper position.

Branch line train

Once at Penarth, the engine would rest; its boiler fit to burst. My mother, brother and I would cross the road, buckets and spades in hand ready for the walk down through what were then very beautiful gardens. There was a fountain somewhere along the route to the beach, with a large basin full of goldfish. We always stopped to look at them.

The descent to the beach was quite steep. Besides flights of normal steps, much of the path consisted (perhaps it still does) of very deep but shallow steps, so deep that it wasn't possible to cover one in a single stride. Instead, we took about two steps to each one and it was just possible to run down them. Usually my brother and I did just this, leaving Mam to walk down and catch us up. The sea beckoned and every second was precious. Who would be the first one to spot the sea?

Steam trains weren't only used by families for holiday excursions. Once a year, at Whitsun, our Baptist Chapel in Clive Street would have its Whitsun treat. We looked forward to this all year and it was a major event in our calendar. Being allowed to participate was dependent upon our attendance at Sunday School throughout the year, an incentive that seemed to work. Bearing in mind that the chapel was attended by hundreds of families, and that it was the home of the scouts, the guides and cubs, besides Bible

The Whitsun Treat lorry departs Baptist Chapel

classes, the Mothers' Union and various other groups, the number of people involved was significant.

Residents along the whole street would stand on their doorsteps cheering and clapping as we, dressed in white shirts for the boys and brightly coloured dresses for the girls, marched two abreast from the chapel to the railway station. We held banners and flags aloft; a band preceded us and two or three lorries containing tents, food, tea urns, tables and chairs, cutlery and all the paraphernalia of a fête, followed behind. The procession was impressive, a sign of the thriving chapel community

Once at Grangetown Station, we climbed the steep flight of steps to the platform which was some height above the road, passing through the clicking turnstile as hundreds of us were counted past the ticket office. Once on the platform and herded into groups, we awaited excitedly and rather noisily for the arrival of the specially chartered train. A particular fear was always that over-excited children would fall off the platform, but this, thankfully, never happened.

The journey was special not only because we didn't need tickets, because they had been paid for by the chapel, but that this train would travel non-stop to our destination, just for us. It was special and we called it just that: 'a special'. The train took us either to Lavernock Station or to Swanbridge Station, both of which were near the coast. In both cases, once arrived we had a march of about a mile, always in formation, to the field where the event would take place.

As we marched from the station, we became increasingly excited, especially when someone shouted that they had seen the sea and we realised we could smell it too. We looked out for the large tents and the central marquee which had been erected by the men the day before. To be able to be part of the team of adults who set up the field was the zenith of our hopes and aspirations. Only men were allowed to do this; it was a rite of passage.

As we waited for the train at Grangetown, the lorries which had been in the procession transporting tables, tea urns, chairs and other paraphernalia, would pass the station and drive straight to the site. It was always a race as to which method of transport would be faster.

Morris 8 (left) and AA motorcycle and sidecar (right)

The drivers of the Whitsun Treat train, some of whom lived in Grangetown, would join in the race to the site, piling on steam to beat the lorries. They would also blow their whistles continually and tried to climb hills as fast as they could. Usually the lorries won, but one particular year they didn't because one of them broke down, which was a common occurrence.

Even if driving an ordinary family car, you had to be something of an amateur mechanic to ensure you were able to carry out repairs on the side of the road. All drivers carried extensive sets of tools and various gadgets for this purpose, including a separate jack with which to lift the car or lorry (they weren't provided by the manufacturer in all cases). It was not unusual to see people repairing a puncture on the side of the road. What little space there was in a car boot was usually filled with such equipment, luggage being a secondary consideration, sometimes having to be carried either on the roof or on a carrier rack added to the boot, whatever the weather.

The advent of the Automobile Association (AA) and the Royal Automobile Club (RAC) brought some relief to those who were not good mechanics. At this time, in the early 50s, both the AA and the RAC mechanics rode around on motorbikes with sidecars full of tools and spare parts.

Whenever a patrolman spotted a member, distinguished by having a chrome-plated badge on the front of the radiator or on the bumper, he would salute. We children riding in the car were constantly on the lookout, in our case for AA men, and would in turn salute them as they passed.

The slightly eccentric uniform always struck me because the patrolmen wore jodhpurs, a type of trousers that were close-fitting below the knee but loose-fitting and flared at the thighs, popular with polo players.

Not all trains were to be encountered running on railways, they were also encountered crossing roads. This seemed very strange because they appeared so much taller, even the small so-called tank engines, when on the same level as a pedestrian or cyclist. Within the docks great care had to be taken when driving, cycling or walking because long trains crossed and re-crossed the roads, often stopping across them to shunt trucks into sidings. They had absolute priority with which no one argued, of course.

An area which is now a retail park was once the route to the small ferry to Penarth and had railway tracks running its whole length, on both sides of the road. The embankment tracks joined up with those at Grangetown Station; those in the Penarth direction led past the Red House pub on the seashore, ending eventually at Penarth Harbour on the Ely river. On these branch lines, mainly oil and petroleum tanks were shunted to and from an Esso petrol depot.

It was impossible to approach engines outside the Red House pub because of a wooden fence, but no such barrier existed along the length of Ferry Road itself. The many sidings there linked the gasworks with other associated businesses, such as The Taff Wagon Company, The Supolstery Ltd (furniture makers where my father worked), Harrison and Barber, horse slaughterers and knackers and Western Trinidad Lake Asphalt Company (a name I always thought exotic and which used tar by-products from the gasworks).

When I was sixteen, I got a job delivering Christmas post to these businesses and I remember most of them. They were generally pretty run-down, dangerous places, where concern for health and safety had not penetrated. Most had vicious guard dogs too.

It was possible to cycle right alongside the moving engines and trains of trucks along Ferry Road as they moved in and out of these sidings delivering materials (sometimes dead horses). The sight of these cadavers was one that shocked and intrigued in equal measure. Their meat would be rendered for feeding to pigs and their bones and hooves made into glue. We could follow shunting operations at close quarters and spent many an hour cycling up and down alongside the engines, accompanying them, talking to the drivers and being warned off by some.

The gasworks owned their own engines. They were small saddle tankers (carrying the water for the engine in curved tanks over the boiler, like saddle bags) and which worked mostly within the confines of the gasworks; but they would need to emerge from time to time to bring in more coal and to bring out ash or tar.

I once rode on one for a few hundred yards within the works, my grandfather having persuaded a friend to let me ride on the footplate. Although this was a very impressionable experience, the engines were not the most interesting things to watch. More interesting by far were the activities of the men shunting wagons into and out of the sidings and making up trains of them, for it was a manual job that needed not only skill but fitness too.

The men responsible had to be fit because they literally ran alongside the moving trucks and with a flick of a long pole with a specially twisted hook on the end, they hooked or un-hooked wagon couplings as the train was moving. I suppose today this would be stopped on safety grounds, but back then it was the only way of doing it.

If, for example, a wagon of tar was wanted at the tar works, a 'shunter' would operate the points by hand, which meant raising a very heavy, weighted lever, painted white, so that the track points changed in the direction of a siding. He then ran back to the approaching train, the engine pushing the wagons from the rear, and as he ran he would wait until the wagon in question, which had to be the foremost of course, had crossed the points and turned into the siding. He would then run alongside the wagon, undo the coupling by

Saddle-tank engine

poking his pole into the gap between the wagon and its neighbours, and signal to the engine driver to stop.

The train would stop, but the loose wagon would carry on down the siding he'd chosen. Now he had to stop it. He did so by running to catch it up and jump onto a long brake lever at the side of the moving wagon so that it came to a stop at the right place. A lot of effort was needed. The engine driver had a much easier time, but they both had to work as a team.

These operations would be accompanied by lots of noise. When the train stopped suddenly, for example, all the trucks still coupled together would snap at their couplings one after the other in a rattling cascade as they were jerked to a halt, domino-fashion. It was then strangely eerie to hear the sole wagon that had been released rolling on its own down the siding: a very satisfying sound as its steel wheels rolled on the steel rails, apparently self-propelled.

When the train, which was at the back of the line of wagons, started up again, it would ram itself into the wagons, causing their spring-loaded buffers to crash into each other, once again making a lovely cascade of noise all the way along the train of trucks as they hit each other. Then, as the full weight of the train was felt by the engine, it would need to push harder and this meant pouring out

Goods train in shunting yards

more steam, accompanied by loud chuffing sounds from the stack as steam and smoke were expelled.

On warm summer evenings, when my bedroom window was wide open, I could often hear such noises coming from the shunting yards, where large numbers of sidings of this type had to be filled with wagons for various train configurations. The cascading crashing of the couplings and the chugging of the straining engines were wonderful sounds by which to fall asleep.

Heavy industrial activities were always accompanied by light from flames and sparks. Street lighting wasn't really necessary in some areas due to the sky being lit up by the flames of industry. There was always a background glow. I remember returning home at night on a train from London in the 1960s. I may have gone there for an interview or similar and it seemed that throughout most of the journey I could pick out where we were by the fires of industry.

Swindon was probably the most illuminated, by the work going on in its huge manufacturing and repair sheds for engines, before we got to the border with Wales. Actually, the light from furnace fires and steel-making was perhaps much brighter when travelling at night on a steam train because the lights in the carriages were extremely dim, being just a small 15 W bulb here and there, without a shade round them, and which barely glowed, its illumination fading and brightening with the changing speed of the engine. Not all the light fittings had managed to hang onto their bulbs either, some passengers believing falsely that the low-voltage bulbs would work at home.

As we neared Newport, its large steel works would light up the sky with sparks flying from the furnaces. Port Talbot has retained this to some extent. When the eponymous Bessemer furnaces are operating, the showers of sparks light up the town. Similarly, flares at the petroleum plants at Baglan Bay, Port Talbot and at Sully, near Barry, once provided spectacular displays.

Even gasworks, which then used coal in the process, provided firework displays of their own. Coal was heated in retorts and once all the gases

Bessemer furnace in action

had been driven off, the red-hot coke that remained had to be cleared out and this was both spectacular as well as noisy.

A steel door would be opened at the back of the coke retort and a ram would push the glowing coke out the front into steel wagons for tipping somewhere. The sight of the red-hot coke being pushed out into the night was fascinating and I would often wait quite some time to be able to witness it.

Heavy industry was very much a man's activity and often a dangerous one. Now, with such industries either gone or much reduced in size, there seems little with which to be impressed, in a physical sense. Wondering at the rapidity of a computer is a purely intellectual appreciation and gives no visceral impact or the sense of awe that a steelworks or a steam engine did. The pounding of an enormous steam hammer was perhaps the ultimate in awe and fear that a young lad could witness, the very ground shuddering beneath his feet.

Painting entitled 'Steelworks, Cardiff at Night' by Lionel Walden

CHAPTER EIGHT

The Glory of Locomotion

By far the most impressive steam engines were the great express engines of the London route. These were the so-called Pacific and Castle Class engines, the last and finest express locomotives to be built at Swindon for the Great Western Railway. I was so struck by their beauty, their power and their engineering, that down some of their characteristics had to be included in this book.

At Canton, to the west of Cardiff, was one of the largest maintenance sheds in the UK. The original site had been built by Brunel to service the engines of his Great Western Railway (also known as 'God's Wonderful Railway'). There is a sense of pride in naming a railway 'The Great Western' that is much better than 'Arriva', I feel.

Brunel, having driven his railway as far as Bristol, was persuaded by the coal and steel masters of South Wales (notably Richard Crawshay of Merthyr) to extend it to Cardiff, to service their huge investments in coal mines, steel works and tin plating works in the valleys. But Brunel died before he could realise this dream and it was up to others to push the line onto Cardiff and eventually to Swansea, Fishguard and Ireland.

An engineer named Richardson built the incredible Severn Tunnel in 1886. At 4.5 miles, it was the longest underwater tunnel in the world at that time, made entirely of bricks, laid in a spiral helix. It made possible a direct link between Bristol and South Wales, saving a 61 mile detour around Gloucester, its *raison d'etre* being entirely founded on coal; passenger traffic was not initially a priority. At its peak, Cardiff was exporting 53 million tons of coal a year, at least a third of it transported through the tunnel, for industry and for the living room fires of London and the Midlands.

The Great Western Railway's Art Deco central station at Cardiff still bears the name of Brunel and Richardson's railway; although the building we see now is the second version of the station, opened in 1934.

Faced in Portland stone, it's a listed building, noted for its architecture as illustrated by its attractive booking hall. It is one of the busiest stations on the UK network. The Canton maintenance sheds are a mile or so to the west of the main station. These had the means of turning around the large express engines on a huge rotating table.

It was at Cardiff, fed from the valleys' mines and steel works via the Taff Vale Railway, that trains would pick up Welsh steam coal, which was every stoker's favourite. This preference was so widespread that steam ships and engines all over the world were using it. In 1910, Cardiff was the world's largest coal port, which made its owner, the Marquess of Bute, the world's richest man.

The Coal Exchange that the Marquiess and others established is now undergoing a resurrection as a hotel, with perhaps space for history societies and other social groups.

Good contact with London was essential to such an important business centre and fast express trains were needed for the run. New engines were designed and built for this specific purpose, giving rise to a generation of mechanical machines the like of which will never be seen again.

A man named Collett was responsible for their design and he lived in Swindon where they were built, but made

Above: Front entrance of Cardiff Central Station

Below: Cardiff Central Station booking hall

frequent journeys to Cardiff to inspect the engines in service and those being maintained at the Canton sheds.

Strictly off-limits to anyone other than those who worked there, especially nine- or ten-year-old boys, the Canton sheds were formidable places to explore; but explore them I did, on several occasions. These huge and powerful engines were the pride of the Great Western and you could see why. Standing on the ground alongside them, they seemed as tall as a house and twice as massive. At that age, I was dwarfed by the main drive wheels, which stood at 6 feet 8 inches in diameter. As for the engines' length, they seemed to go on and on. They were actually 73 feet long.

The huge boiler, 22 feet long and 5 feet in diameter, was only part of the monster. Besides the spacious cab (a feature beloved of train drivers) the engine pulled a tender full of coal and water, enough to take the engine and its train the 200 miles to London without refuelling. They could take on water at speed via a clever water trough in the centre of some portions of the track, notably to the west of Swindon. Weighing 89 tons (unladen) and pulling 540 tons at an average of 80 mph, these were the finest engines ever produced. For the first time, they employed super-heated or dry steam.

The engine had four 'bogey' wheels in the front and three pairs of massive drive wheels. It was thus known as a 4-6-0 locomotive. The tender had six sets of wheels. It was a version of these locomotives, The Mallard, which set the world speed record for steam in 1938, by travelling at 126 mph, a record that has never been broken. That engine is now preserved at the National Railway Museum in York.

In spite of their immense power and speed, they were very streamlined and beautiful machines, distinguished by a slight taper from the front of the firebox, to the front of the boiler. Immediately in front of the cab the sides were flat.

The first such engine to make its appearance at Cardiff's sheds was the King George V and she was one of the last to be decommissioned in the 1960s. Its lovely dark green colour was a background to fine gold lines that picked out the various contours of the boiler, cab and gearing. Brass hoops engirdled the boiler; even the cab was lined with brass edging.

A notable feature, which the Americans liked apparently, (they were so impressed by these engines they bought them in large numbers) was the copper top to its stack. A coat of arms was emblazoned on the sides of the tender and the whole 'rig' shone. What a difference to the dirty, grubby diesels we have now. These machines were something to be proud of and gave rise to large numbers of people gathering at stations to see them: the original train spotters, of which I was one.

It was the huge drive links on the main drive wheels which always impressed me; for their size, their condition and their function. When I think that they, and they alone, had to transmit enough power from the pistons to the wheels to pull an express train of perhaps 10 or 11 carriages at about 80 mph, they are objects to be respected. The power they transmitted, the speed with which they moved and the precision with which these huge pieces of steel were made, were characteristics which, to an engineer, are inspiring.

The first time I got into the sheds, by squeezing through a gap in the corrugated iron walls, one of these leviathans was being backed into a bay for cleaning and maintenance. This meant firstly

Coal Exchange building, now the Exchange Hotel

emptying its firebox and then purging the boiler of steam. Both activities were done by hand. The fire was very deep and still very much alive and had to be removed by using a long-handled steel scraper pushed into the firebox and pulled out so as to draw the fire into a trap beneath, from which it fell into a steel trough. This was accompanied by lots of smoke and sparks of course.

The purging of the boiler was deafening! Opening the valves of the boiler released literally tons of water in the form of super-heated, high pressure steam which escaped with an horrendous noise and which continued for a long time, about half an hour in fact. The steam filled the shed, trying to escape as best it could out of louvres in the roof, but initially most of it collected in clouds inside. From these two activities one got a first-hand, almost visceral, measure of the power bottled up inside this giant.

The men maintaining and driving these monsters were proud of their work and what they could achieve. They were also long-standing employees who had worked their way up in the trade of railwaymen. For example, in order to become a driver, a man would first have to spend years as a stoker, a hard physical job, often requiring two men; then he may be lucky to become an assistant driver on short routes and eventually be promoted to be 'king of the railways', an express driver.

As a matter of interest, the French word *chauffeur* does not mean driver; it derives from the verb *chauffer*, to heat. So a chauffeur is really a *stoker*, he who heats the engine.

Their jobs were stable and secure and they were proud and happy men, admired by their colleagues and respected by their neighbours as people of great responsibility, like captains of a ship.

The way they looked after the engines was like watching someone with a new car. They were always oiling and greasing them, which was very important, and polishing the paintwork, the steel linkages, piston rods and the extensive brass work. The most obvious brass work was a lovely rail which was fixed to either side of the boiler, to which the driver would cling when needing to exit his cab and walk towards the front of the engine.

In the Canton sheds, it was possible to see not just one of these glorious machines but several. If one goes to the National Rail Museum in York (the site of George and Robert Stephenson's very first engine manufacturing works in 1817) you will get an idea of how impressive these machines are and the huge scale of them.

As a passenger, it wasn't only the majesty of the engines which impressed. Aboard, even in Standard Class, one was cosseted. The style and comfort with which trains carried their passengers have been completely lost. Not only was the seating spacious and comfortable but if you wanted a meal, there was a separate restaurant car available on the service to London.

Here is a contemporary description of the lovely brown and cream restaurant cars which these engines pulled:

"These are undoubtedly the most handsome stock on this nation's railways today. Panelled in finest walnut, fitted with the best Wilton carpets, with windows shaded by silk damask curtains of the most subtle shades, the finest covers grace the tables where china, glassware and cutlery are of the most exquisite. They provide a standard of luxury and comfort which will not be surpassed."

(Western Mail, 1951)

I have a book that shows the menus of the day (1940) as costing 3/- (three shillings or 15p) for lunch and 4/- (20p) for dinner. Each meal was of three courses with tea or coffee and even if you only wanted a cup of tea, the restaurant car would oblige you and would charge just 3d (<1p).

* * *

The large railway engines and their moving parts were as nothing compared with those that powered ships, such as the pleasure boats which ploughed between Cardiff and various ports on the Severn Estuary, one of which, The Waverley, is still running, although it is not a paddle steamer. Originally, four such paddle steamers were running regularly from Cardiff to Penarth, Barry and thence across to Weston-Super-Mare, Ilfracombe, Minehead and Bristol. Sometimes, one or other of them would also offer a cruise for a day, visiting Lundy Island or the Flat Holm island.

They were wide ships with a very shallow draft; so much so that they were put into service during the war as mine-sweepers, suitably camouflaged. Some had two funnels, always painted white, and were part of The White Funnel Fleet. Their paddles made them rather elegant and very unusual. They had been built in the 1930s and offered a pretty good day out.

We used to walk to the docks, queue alongside what is now a restaurant (it was then the pilots' office) and enter the port past what is now a large pub. This was excitement indeed. Once aboard and having quickly explored where the amenities were, we settled into a seat either on deck (preferably) or if the weather wasn't so good, below decks in the spacious lounges.

Watching the seamen at work was fascinating, especially watching them handling the huge ropes which tied the ship to the dock. Casting off was simple: the steam-driven winches were engaged at either end of the ship and once enough slack had been put into the ropes, they were simply slid off their quayside moorings and cast into the sea. The winches were then reversed and the rope pulled in, dripping with water. All this water came aboard as the men wrapped the rope into coils on the deck.

Docking was a much more interesting and skilful procedure, requiring that a lightweight rope be thrown first from the ship to the dockside, where someone would (mostly) catch it. The light rope being attached to the huge hawser, it would then be let over the side of the ship and hauled in by hand onto the dock.

Winches would let off steam as they strained to pull in the heavy rope and gradually tighten it, pulling the whole ship gently against the dockside. Since the rope had been in the sea, it was full of water,

Campbell White Funnel paddle steamer

which would be progressively squeezed out as the tension increased, with a steady moaning sound as the rope tightened within itself.

The gangway would be let down onto the dock, but it was not always easy to negotiate. Depending on the height of the tide and therefore the height of the ship against the dockside, the gangway was often not level; so at the ship end, it could project upwards and old people especially had to be helped over this obstacle before being helped down the sometimes slippery gangway to dry land.

So besides the pleasure of the cruise, watching as the paddles beat their rhythm into the sea, leaving a foaming wake, there were technical manoeuvres to watch too. But the most exciting thing to observe were the engines. The constructors of these ships had built a public viewing gallery in the engine room, where passengers could stand above the engines and observe them.

They were single cylinder steam engines but because of the diameter of the paddles – perhaps 15 feet or so – they had to have a lot of leverage to be able to push the paddles round. So the most impressive part of them was the huge (perhaps 20 feet long) steel shafts that transmitted the power from the pistons to the paddles via a huge crank shaft.

They moved in and out of the pistons of course, but also had an up and down movement as the crank dictated, so the ends of these shafts were not only moving at high speed along the axis of the ship but also up and down as the paddles moved in a circle. If the ship described a sharp turn, it would naturally roll, so that one of the paddles would be deeper in the water than the other and more steam had to be piled onto that one to make up for the loss in power. Then the whole ship shuddered under the unbalanced application of power.

The noise in the engine room was deafening and the air filled with the lovely smells of hot oil, grease and steam. Such engines give the observer a visceral sense of what steam power is. It's such a pity that young people have no experience of such things.

CHAPTER NINE

Horses and Carts

There was still a surprising amount of horse-drawn transport when I was young. It was an economic form of transport for small businesses, if slow.

Some of these businesses were on the margins of society, such as the rag and bone man for example, but horses were still around and the most significant user of them in Cardiff was the Hancocks Brewery which was then behind the central station and which is now owned by Brains.

Hancocks continued using horses for pulling their drays in Cardiff for some years and kept a stable of shire horses for this purpose. Outside the city, horses were not viable of course because of the distance involved and the time it would take, but within the city they were a striking advertisement for the brewery.

Rag and bone man

We didn't have to be told that the dray had arrived at the Catholic Club at the end of our street; we could hear the heavy clip clop of the hooves of these enormous horses as they moved along Corporation Road and turned slowly into our street. The club's cellar entrance was on our street and therefore the arrival of the dray allowed us not only to look with wonder at these animals but also to study how the men were able to off-load such enormous wooden barrels with relative ease.

The most striking impression of these animals was one of sheer size. They were huge; the dray they pulled was huge; the barrels were huge. They had feet as large as dinner plates, covered with long hair. When they arrived, the driver would not only apply the brake of the wagon, or dray, but also place on the ground in front of the horses a heavy iron weight to which he attached a rope clipped to the bridle of one of them to keep them from moving away. If you were lucky, you could get permission to hold on to this length of rope as if holding the horses single-handed. What a great feeling as a small lad to peer up into these horses' lovely eyes, albeit half hidden with blinkers.

In spite of their imposing size and obvious strength, the horses were touchingly docile. After their exertion, they would suddenly snort, which would be a little frightening, but otherwise they were calm and extremely patient.

One horse in particular, who used to be the second horse in terms of pecking order had a habit of lifting his left front leg and planting it on the road so that only the front tip of his shoe was in contact with the road. It looked as though he was posing nonchalantly. It was his own method of resting his leg, but he only did this once he had had his feed and finished his round of snorting and lifting his head up and down so as to shake the feed sack. The driver usually fixed this feed bag around his head to make sure he and his partner had enough energy for the rest of the round.

Horse-drawn brewery dray

The wagon was enormous and it had to be. It carried probably two dozen wooden barrels, each containing perhaps 50 gallons of beer. This was a huge weight. The wheels were entirely beneath it, so that the chassis or base of the wagon was quite high. This was also important for the horses, so that the shafts of the wagon were on a level with their saddles. Chains and leather traces of all kinds festooned the horses' backs and were fixed at various points to the shafts. The horses wore decorative brasses, had saddles which were also decorated, and with tall brass rods which stuck up above the saddle and carried bells. The wagon itself was variously red or dark green with thin gold lines picking out the profiles.

The driver would be seated on his bench, with his partner, both wearing very long leather aprons down to their feet, the driver's feet placed on an inclined board. This is just how coaches centuries ago were designed, so that the driver was effectively half standing and had somewhere to push against with his feet if he needed to pull on the reins; otherwise the horses could pull him from his seat.

To top off the dray, Hancocks had erected a painted sign which was on top of a frame which was above the driver's head. The overall height of the thing was therefore significant. The reins were of course very long and I always wondered how a single pair of hands could manage all of them and be able to direct individual horses so accurately. A long whip, placed upright alongside the driver completed the outfit.

To get the barrels off this wagon and safely into the cellar was the task in hand. They were large handmade oak barrels, with steel edges, very much larger than modern ones. I suppose they were about 3 feet high. To get your hands between one of these and a wall when the barrel was moving would mean the loss of a hand. So expertise and care were essential.

The technique consisted of placing a very large, heavy, woven hemp cushion on the ground, beneath the barrel to be off-loaded, so that when it dropped, its fall would be broken but it wouldn't bounce – otherwise this could be dangerous. One man would carefully topple a barrel from the wagon whilst the other effectively 'caught' it by its end as it hit the cushion. Then both would assist in rolling the full barrel towards the cellar entrance.

Now this is the clever bit. Firstly, two oak runners were positioned in the cellar, with one end at the pavement level and the other on the floor of the cellar. They would be spaced in such a way that the barrel's belly would touch the floor first and slow it down a little, so the runners were at a slight angle to each other and wider at the bottom than the top. This meant that as the barrel rolled down, its centre of gravity would sink. Two ropes were passed around the barrel whilst it was on the pavement and then it was pushed towards the two runners, running out the ropes slowly so that the barrel could begin to run down the runners.

Great care and strength were required to do this. If one man's grip slipped on the rope, the barrel would skew around and rush down the runners and possibly smash; or worse, it would career into the poor cellar man down there. So they used leather 'cloths' with which they cupped the ropes in their hands to improve their grip whilst allowing it to run through their hands without burning them.

Once at the bottom, the barrel would be handled by the cellar man and his assistant and the ropes reclaimed for the next barrel. Any empty barrels would have been lifted up first of course and stacked on the road ready to be loaded and taken away. These, like the full ones, were of the traditional shape. Their bulbous shape is inherently unstable and all barrels had to be carefully wedged in place on the dray before moving off, using oak wedges and a sound blow from a hammer.

Once all was finished, the feed bags would be removed from the horses and the ropes and weights lifted onto the wagon. Both driver and mate would climb way up into their high seats, sort out the various reins and traces and release the brake. Then you could really feel the power of these beautiful beasts and how tolerant they were, working hard all day without a murmur of complaint. For us bystanders there was usually a bonus from one or other of the horses, which they left in the road for my bucket and spade to scoop up for my grandfather's roses.

Delivering beer barrels from a dray

CHAPTER TEN
Bombs

Our island, being close to the docks and having a gasworks in its midst, was hit by a number of stray bombs during the war, notably in 1941. The buildings so destroyed, rather than being scenes of sadness, were exciting playgrounds for we who played on them after the war.

An incendiary bomb landed quite close to us, falling on Hollywell's Bakery. The site is now a hardware shop. Sadly, the baker and all his family were killed (thirty-two people in all), and the incendiary bomb destroyed their house and most of the bakery; but

Bomb site

it left intact the stables and the open-fronted, brick cart sheds built as alcoves, in which the baker's carts were kept.

In one of these, a beautiful yellow trap remained, completely intact, its shafts pointing expectantly downwards like a dog greeting its owner. It was complete with traces and a saddle which hung upon pegs on the wall to its left. It was the vehicle from which the baker had once delivered his produce; but for us it was a wonderful play thing with which to let our imaginations roam.

The large wheels were interesting: they were so slender and elegant, contrasting with the rough axle head protruding from the centre of them, itself wrapped in tight bands of steel.

The seat was of leather but well worn, with a straw-like filling visible through tears in the fabric. The back of the seat was a simple but quite comfortable padded wooden plank, supported on springy steel supports. Behind it, wooden seats either side, over the wheels, completed the fittings except for the large mud guards which always seemed to me too far from the wheels to do any good. There was a smart little door at the very back through which passengers passed and which shut with a nice brass catch.

It was surprisingly light in weight and delicately balanced about its large wheels. This meant that two boys could get between the shafts, lift them and move the cart fairly easily across the cobbled courtyard, which was still intact and relatively clear of debris. With a few girls in the back this was great fun, but difficult to move backwards again into the cart's alcove. So we often just let go of the shafts and the girls fell out! For short people such as children, this presented a problem, because the shafts were then left sticking up in the air and unreachable. So we had to get some help and right the cart by lifting its back, which had much less leverage of course.

Site of the Hollyman's Bakery

The ovens of the bakery were relatively intact, one of them at least. Being made of arched brickwork, they were strong and resisted the force of the explosion I suppose. We sometimes dared each other to lie inside one whilst the iron door was shut. Usually, this was a signal for your friends to run off and hide, hoping to make you panic inside.

A particularly sad reminder that this had once been a home was the sight of one of the upstairs fireplaces still intact and attached high up on the wall of the house next door. Seeing such a private domestic item stuck like that, so high up and on such public display, felt indecent, somehow. But it reminded us that this was actually a scene of sadness.

Below in the yard, piles of rubble obliterated any shape of the original house and bakery, but there was the occasional doorway and lots of broken china and slates. The bomb, being an incendiary device, consumed the whole building with fire, leaving very little behind.

Where walls had not completely been broken down, their jagged, brick-edged profiles acted as steps up which to climb and be daring, sometimes with a good, hard fall to follow. Most times we returned home pretty dirty from this bomb site but it held a fascination for us for many a year until it was built upon.

The very notion of what a bomb might be also fascinated us. Some boys bragged that they knew where there was one, still unexploded, but couldn't tell anyone where, because it was too dangerous to approach. Fathers, returning from the war provided feedstock for stories about bombs, ammunition and lucky escapes. All our fathers were of course heroes, it was just a matter of agreeing which one was the greatest. Stories, mostly fed by vivid imaginations, abounded. 'Did you hear the one about Alun's father? He was so brave he doesn't like to talk about it.'

My father, a diminutive lorry driver (he was barely 5 feet tall) with the Royal Signals, (a part of the army which provided battlefield communications) was difficult to make into the greatest hero of all and I sometimes felt at a disadvantage. Dad's height didn't seem to impress the other boys. But they began to take more of an interest in his military career when they and I realised that he was demobilised ('de-mobbed') much later than most others in the Armed Forces. Surely, he must be important for this to happen! (Or what had he done that was so bad?)

The European theatre of war ended in 1945, but he was not released immediately. He and others like him were needed to repair the telephone systems of mainland Europe and so they worked on. Although he had served an apprenticeship at the Tudor Joinery, a small business in the corner of what was Temperance Town (now the bus station and all the buildings up to the Millennium Stadium), and was therefore a carpenter/cabinet maker by trade, his skills in the army's telephone systems were to serve him well after the war.

In the early 50s, his chair-making employer (the Supolstery Co in Ferry Road) went out of business and after a miserable time looking for work, he got a job with 'God's Poor Orphans', the General Post Office or GPO. It was then he discovered that he had been adopted and that his name was actually not Noyes - which was really his third Christian name - but Bone. After some legal wrangles over false declarations, etc., he changed his name by Deed Poll to Noyes in 1953.

This was a great surprise when it was revealed to me after Dad's funeral. It was also indicative of what was a rather secretive society years ago. I think many a family had secrets; often to do with illegitimate offspring, divorces and similar relational issues. Such secrets were the domain of adults only, who went to enormous lengths to avoid them leaking out, even, in my case, to close family members.

Supolstery Works, Ferry Road

Employers had to keep open the jobs of returning soldiers and the Supolstery Company in Ferry Road did just that, but business was poor. People after the war could not afford hand-made furniture and materials were scarce.

For about a year around 1951, he cast about looking for work. He set himself up in business in the loft of what had been a small stable, such as the one shown below, but that too failed to attract sufficient clients to keep him going.

I used to work with him from time to time at his small business premises, although it was not the place for a six or seven year-old: nails and tacks were all over the floor and the steps down from the loft to the (cobbled) stable were unguarded.

It was my job to gather up old chair coverings if I could, including the tacks and the old horse hair padding and canvas webbing as he repaired the wooden frames and re-stuffed and covered furniture. He was fascinating to watch. As with any tradesman who knows his stuff and has been working at it for years, he seemed to work without effort and without thinking. He worked so fast that it was difficult to keep up with him if he needed my help. One of the tricks of his trade, which always made my eyes pop when he did it, was how he never needed to break off from his work to pick up new tacks. It was because he had them in his mouth.

Before beginning a new phase of work, he would take a handful of small tacks and throw them into his mouth as though they were peanuts. Somehow, he could produce one at a time, with the head first, just when he needed one. This meant both hands were free for pulling and positioning the material he was working on.

Stable and yard

The materials used were strange, with a smell and texture all their own. He would have rolls of 'Rexine' a material in various colours which imitated leather; there would be various rolls of 'moquette' too, a patterned cloth which was very hard wearing. Then there would be my favourite plaything, huge rolls (perhaps 9 inches in diameter) of canvas webbing for making seats. There were also large sacks of padding and filling: horse hair, cotton wadding, kapok and flock. Another detail I remember was taking delivery of a sack (everything came in sacks) of chair springs and trying to untangle them – it was not so easy.

The tools of the trade were unusual, in particular a device with hinged handles like pincers, but at the mouth of which were mating rectangular blocks with serrated faces. This gadget was used to grip material, especially canvas webbing, and pull it tight against a wooden chair frame.

Another tool he used a lot was an enormous pair of upholsterers' scissors with which he could cut out a sheet of, say, Rexine, in seconds, just by looking at the shape he needed. I shan't go into the details of how to repair furniture but suffice it to say the process was fascinating and I spent many an hour watching and trying to help in 'men's work'.

In spite of his low overheads, Dad couldn't make his business pay and he had to stop. He even spent an agonising period as a furnace labourer at a brick works. The work was backbreaking for a small chap and he often returned home completely covered in brick dust, especially in his hair. One day I remember being in the lane around lunch time to see him peddling home unexpectedly early. He told me he'd had enough and had walked out.

Mam was really worried. Once someone walked away from a job, they might find it difficult to find another.

***

Bombs were also things we used to make. We discovered that shops sold ready-made explosives in the form of 'caps'. I don't know if they are still made, but they were rolls of paper, brown on one side, red on the other, and between these two layers, blobs of gunpowder were sealed. If struck, a blob or cap, would explode. They were made in rolls which would fit into the bullet chamber of a toy gun

Toy gun

Explosive caps for toy gun

and made quite a realistic bang, essential for any self-respecting cowboy in those days.

We thought that to make a bomb, we had to achieve two things: make a loud noise; and make a mess. The former we did by using the gunpowder from caps, either by splitting the papers and pouring out the powder, or more safely, to just use the caps themselves. We then took two large bolts and a nut (the bigger and heavier the better) and screwed one bolt half way into the nut, leaving a space between the end of the bolt and the top of the nut.

Placing caps or a charge of our recovered gunpowder into this space and then gently screwing the second bolt into the nut formed a perfect bomb. The gunpowder would be compressed anyway by the bolts and if we threw this device high into the air, over a concrete or tarmac surface, the resulting impact would set off the gunpowder. Having nowhere to go, the explosive gases could only force themselves out around any spare play on the thread, so producing a very loud bang indeed.

As for making a mess, we experimented with this device to dislodge masonry, especially the old lime-based stonework evident in various Victorian walls up and down the lane, noticeably in the walls of the stable block directly behind our house. This building, used to house horses for many years, had external walls which were made from large, natural stones, so that in places the lime mortar was fairly wide and asking to be blasted out.

One day we decided to give it a try. We found a suitable stone surrounded by friable mortar pointing and inserted one end of one of our 'bombs' into a hole we made in the pointing. Then one of us was volunteered to give the thing a great whack with a hammer to see what would happen. What happened scared us so much we never attempted it again! The explosion was loud alright, but it just threw the hammer out of the hand of the striker and hurled it against the wall of our house, narrowly missing those who were watching.

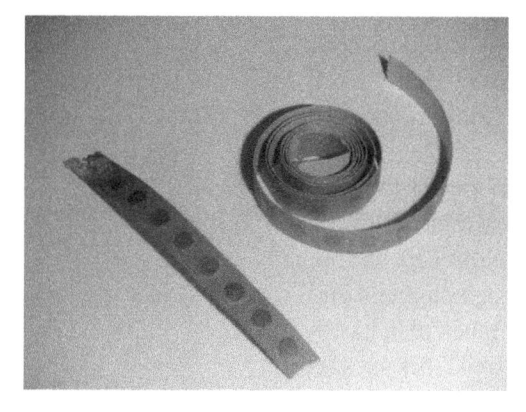

So we found other ways of making a mess: by playing at low tide in the mud of the River Taff. We found that these extensive stretches of tidal mud were great for investigating how boulders would impact on the mud when hurled into it. The thrill of the exercise lay in seeing not only how scarily the boulders would sink without trace, but also how far from the impact site they could throw the mud. Given enough momentum, most of the ejected mud would be thrown forward and then it was a question of devising a game to see who could develop their technique so as to project most mud furthest.

We also tried similar techniques on mounds of red-hot semi-molten slag behind the gasworks. Every so often, the ovens in which the coal had been 'cooked' in order to produce town gas (and other chemicals, such as tar, sulphur and even the constituents for Nylon) would become contaminated with metals and mineral impurities, small amounts of which, including Uranium, are always present in coal.

This molten slag would be scraped from the retorts and dumped in a glowing volcanic heap at the back of the gasworks. Throwing boulders into this when very fresh and hot would break the thin, dark crust and suddenly reveal the glowing liquid slag beneath, which would shoot out in all directions.

Once we felt that a mound of slag had cooled enough to form a thick crust, tested by throwing a brick at it, we even rode our bikes across it, producing clouds of burning rubber as our tyres briefly caught fire, which is quite silly when one thinks about it. But speed was the secret; we didn't hesitate. One boy got burned doing it, as he stupidly decided to cross the volcano slowly, so that his tyres burst into flames. He then committed a further act of stupidity by putting down his foot to stop himself falling. His shoe and his sock briefly caught fire. Explaining that away to his parents was a work of genius! We scolded him for his timidity by riding across the mound too slowly.

Although I was too young to have any memories of the war, echoes of it remained as part of childhood. For example, Currans' Steel Works, a company operating on the banks of the Taff, used to use its air raid siren as a means of sounding the beginning and end of shifts. It did so for many years. I never thought much of it, just as I didn't question hearing foghorns out at sea, or ships' horns; it was just a part of the atmosphere. Thinking about it now, it seems very odd to use an air raid siren just after a war, and wonder what those who had lived through the bombing must have felt about hearing it again.

During the war, the government encouraged everyone to produce as much food for themselves as possible and my grandfather, being a keen and expert gardener, produced large amounts from two adjacent allotments on the banks of the River Ely, a lovely spot. The allotments allowed him to practice an almost industrial scale of production, aided by large quantities of pigs' manure from the immediately adjacent piggery.

He laid out the allotment very systematically and because the (then) country lanes were often invaded by gypsies looking for food, he made sure the least appetising vegetables, such as spuds, were nearest the dirt lane. Even so, he always feared finding his allotment ravaged by people looking for an easy way of getting food. The worst thing they did was not only to dig up and steal a large quantity of vegetables, but went on to flatten and wreck his large and very beautiful flower section.

He grew amazing flowers, complete with the fine filigree gypsophila used for decorating bouquets; so that when he returned home of an evening with bags bulging with veg, he also brought bunches of flowers for the house and for sale, made up as bouquets.

I remember one year giving him a hand to lay up the first trench of beans. A trench a foot deep was cut and then most of it filled with well-rotted manure from a huge pile which was stacked on the right hand side of the allotment, near the entrance; another pile of fresh manure and rotting vegetable matter

Allotment shed

was on the left, all very systematic. Then we got lengths of rusty one-inch steel piping and used them to make a frame for the beans to climb. It was a heavy structure, but never gave in to the wind.

In the middle of the allotment was a tool shed, not unlike the one illustrated, that leaned at a severe angle - the leaning shed of Pisa. Its single door on the river side was secured by a large lock; he was rather keen on locking things up. I can still smell the earth floor and the old tools inside it. There were very few if any pesticides or fungicides then, so all he used on plants to protect them was Jeye's Fluid, a tar-based treatment with a pleasant (I think) smell. So the musty old shed had a very natural smell, unlike modern garden sheds which contain strong chemicals.

Behind the shed, was a rusty oil drum that was used as a water butt. It was always full of insect life which was fascinating to watch. It was around the water butt that my grandfather grew his mint, which likes moisture and a little shade.

The soil at the allotment was a fine, black river loam, wonderfully productive under his hand. To give an idea of its size, each year he would grow eight rows of climbing beans alone. These would produce enough for us as a family and plenty to sell, which my grandmother did.

She seemed to have a particular affinity with money, her parents and herself once being shopkeepers. Lots of neighbours used to come and buy the veg, which was weighed out on a fairly large set of balance scales in the back yard. The taste of fresh food was glorious, not to be found now unless you also keep your own garden.

I'm not sure if my grandfather welcomed me being with him when gardening. He was a quiet, reticent man, who liked to get on with things and do them well. So having a young lad with him (I had my own miniature set of garden tools he had made me) may have been something he tolerated rather than encouraged, although to be fair to him he never refused to let me come with him.

One of the problems having me around was not only my constant questioning (I expect) but also the comparatively tiny size of my bike. To be accurate, it was not *my* bike which was an odd size (albeit only my first second-hand one at 18 inches) it was *his* bike. He had an enormous machine the like of which I hadn't seen before or since.

I have no idea where it came from, because it was extremely high and there was no way he could touch the floor when he came to a stop. Instead, he had to get off by jumping. Getting on was also difficult: he had to scoot along for some distance before climbing aboard. On the way back from the allotment he would then load the thing with at least three large, green canvas bags full of vegetables using its carrier and the handlebars. How he didn't have an accident with it I don't know. His giant bike remains a mystery to me.

The most exciting part of working on his allotment was going to the piggery next door to collect barrow-loads of manure. Besides the stench, the pigs were not particularly friendly and neither were the three Alsatian guard dogs. I was always anxious that these beasts might break loose and never trusted their attachments when they were tied up. But getting stuck into that manure was good fun; it was smelly and sticky but fun.

Many a back yard contained an interesting play thing inherited from the war, an Anderson air raid shelter. These were half-buried shelters with a semi-circular roof of corrugated iron like the one shown. Inside, was an earth floor and room for about six adults sitting on a plank either side. The doorway was down three steps and was covered in our case by an old rug. They were, of course, very damp and could even fill with rainwater.

Anderson air raid shelter

These things remained for quite some time before the steel roof was needed for steel production and were recalled for melting down. Iron ore, which largely came from abroad was in short supply. During the war itself, iron was even more scarce and most of the iron railings in front of people's houses, including ours and even our gate, were seized by the authorities to melt down and make steel for the war. The holes left after such railings were removed can still be seen today, even on some public buildings, such as the National Museum of Wales in the city centre. Even household iron pots and pans were given up for this same purpose and aluminium, for aeroplanes, was as precious as gold.

The weekly cry from the rag and bone man reminded me of the desperate need in the late 40s and early 50s for clothing (for making paper), for iron and even wood. He used to come around the lanes with his horse and cart and would offer a few pennies or a gold fish for whatever people would give him. Sometimes, his business wasn't strictly honest. His cart was quite high, and by standing on the driving board he could look over walls into back yards, able to spot anything that might be of value. I was often told to go and stand in the yard to make sure he didn't just open the lane door and help himself.

I suppose that in many ways, our society was as efficient as it could be. Nothing, but nothing, was wasted. Even scraps of food from our plates were scraped into a bin at the bottom of the yard – the 'swill bin' – and the contents collected by pig farmers with their horse and cart once a week to feed to their pigs. Clothes were patched and mended, as were shoes. We, like most families, had a shoe-repairer's 'last' on which we repaired our shoes and made sure they would last as long as possible; although there were at least three cobblers in our area too.

Even newspapers were kept for reuse as toilet paper. When running low, we'd tear the papers into rectangles and thread some string through them and hang them in the loo. The best time of year for toilet paper was when tomatoes and oranges came into season because they would arrive at the greengrocers packed with tissue paper and it was a race to get to the shop before it was all snatched up for use in the toilets of Grangetown.

Chickens were also kept. Some of our neighbours had a handful in cages in the yard. I once had to clear out one of these as a 'bob-a-job' task. Although I was paid something measly, the task left me in quite a sorry state and the smell was awful, so I usually left the chicken-clearing customers until last when on my money-raising rounds for our troupe of cubs. Best to start with the old ladies who want you to go and shop for them or polish some brass and then move on to the chicken shed later.

Although bombs and their effect had a tangible effect on our lives, the overall feeling at that time was one of pride, thankfulness and confidence in surviving the war. The UK was after all still the world's first superpower, ruling via its colonies and dominions more than sixty countries. Its shipping fleet and especially its navy was the largest in the world (even compared with the USA) and its institutions were acknowledged to be amongst the best.

Before the war and for a short time after it, the pound was the world's reference currency as is the dollar now; and it was the bank's reserves of gold which supported the pound. Gold was even used as part of our coinage, sovereigns still being legal tender. My grandfather used to save regularly, putting gold sovereigns into a steel strong-box under his bed. "As safe as the Bank of England" was a phrase much used.

Even in the 50s, at least until Suez in 1956, the UK was unchallenged in occupying the moral and political high ground, having sacrificed so much to rescue Europe. Interestingly, it was possibly that very fact which determined various British governments not to join the European Iron and Steel Federation which became the Common Market. As Churchill said, 'Given a free choice between joining with people we have had to rescue because of their capitulation to Fascism, and looking to the open sea, I'll take the open sea.'

And Fascism wasn't finished of course. Spain was still under a dictator, Greece was too. Big changes were to come in the Middle East once Israel was inserted into Palestine (it was the Russians who tipped the vote in the UN over this, we abstained) which has caused so much distress ever since. But at this time, Britain had many allies all over the world, not least of all in the Arab world. The Shah of Persia was still on the throne; we had just returned Egypt to its people and many Arab countries were very close to us, having been occupied as part of the empire, or we having rescued them from attack.

My stamp collection reflected these changes, with names such as Aden, Basutoland, Bechuanaland, British Honduras, Ceylon, the Cook Islands, Gold Coast, Borneo, Malaya, Rhodesia, Sarawak, Tanganyika, and Zanzibar. But examining maps of these countries, one could already see that the carving up by Britain and France in 1919 of what was once Arabia and the rest of the Middle East, had created unnatural 'countries'. Straight lines that cut through the deserts, ignoring traditional tribal territories, was bound to cause tension. These tensions continue today.

CHPTER ELEVEN

Salt, Vinegar, Knives and Umbrellas

The late 50s saw a lot of change in the home. Domestic machinery suddenly burst upon the scene and by the mid-60s the world looked a different place.

Over the period of about a decade, our society transitioned from a post-Victorian one to a consumerist society, bringing with it the promise of unlimited ease and pleasure, most of it led by discoveries in science and engineering. If you were a graduate in science or engineering, industries would beg you to join them. You could name your price.

Washing machines were perhaps the earliest devices to change our lives. Previously, the washing had to be done by hand, heating up water using a coal fire and drying clothes partially by squeezing them in a roller mangle turned by hand and then hanging them out to dry. To be able to wash clothes for a family required a lot of strength and stamina doing it that way.

Washing machine and roller

For our family of six, my mother used to work an entire day, always on Mondays, to wash our clothes. Now we saw that a machine could pretty well do it all and without the attendant mess. The back kitchen was literally awash during washing day and both my mother and grandmother wore waterproof aprons and rubber boots to protect them.

Other machines followed of course and domestic technology was born. Vacuum cleaners had been on the market for a long time, but the kitchen now became the focus of innovation. Gadgets were appearing which promised to make life easier and more leisurely, allowing women to consider getting jobs and having careers of their own.

Then, in around 1950, came the television to Cardiff. TV systems had been in London before the war, in the 30s, but suddenly masts were constructed for a national television system which would reach most of the population. In 1953, the year of the Queen's Coronation, many homes got a television set for the first time, used to watch her crowning. Those who didn't have a set went into their neighbours' houses to watch.

The very first television I saw was a nine-inch one in brown Bakalite. It belonged to our local grocer who was a wartime friend of my father's. He had installed it high up on a shelf so as to catch a signal, but it was so small and so far away it was difficult to see.

We had an enormous television made by Phillips. It had a tiny 14 inch screen (smaller than the average laptop computer now) within a cabinet which must have measured about 18 inches wide by about 24 inches deep and 2 feet tall. It was very large, heavy and resided within a dark veneered wood cabinet. All televisions were considered items of furniture and therefore had to be encased in wood.

The TV picture was, of course, black and white. The aerial was atop the set and had to be turned to face the best transmitter. But the picture quality was poor, even when the 'frame hold' worked or stripes and zig-zag lines didn't appear on the thing. Being valve devices, the sets became hot and subject to rapid ageing, the glowing valves sometimes becoming a little loose, so that a good thump with the hand on the side of the set sometimes put things right. Swearing was also tried, but seemed particularly ineffective at improving the picture, although it occasionally improved the mood of the swearer.

Every so often the transmission would be interrupted for technical reasons. The gap in a programme would be filled by either a static picture of some scene or other, or, more often, a short film of something, such as a potter making a pot on a wheel accompanied by music. 'Intervals' were frustrating but frequent.

Gliding swans on a lake was another gap-filler. Having breaks in transmission was something we had to get used to, which contrasts starkly with our present-day reaction if the Internet slows down. We're probably phoning our provider within minutes. We have become very used to technology not letting us down. When I was young, technology itself was a new concept and felt to be experimental, so we had to be patient and cut the engineers some slack.

The Coronation represented a definite change in our society. The ancient ceremony was viewed for the very first time by millions on the new-fangled television. The ordinary man and woman had effectively been allowed into Westminster Abbey for the first time in 1,000 years. We could witness this ancient ceremony without having to be a member of the elite in society.

It was a very bold statement about the breaking down of class barriers. We saw too that the Queen wasn't only stepping up to a life of luxury and privilege but to a life of duty – there's that important word again. The ceremony required her to make a covenant with God that she would protect her realm and do her duty; something she continues, I think, to live out. It was the representatives of the church who crowned her, not those of the state. She remains, to my mind, a fine example of the values we then enjoyed.

We didn't have a television set in time for the state funeral of King George VI, but I collected a number of photographs and articles from newspapers which I still have in my children's scrap book, something many children kept.

The creation of more and more domestic ease, meant that gradually people became more pre-occupied with building up a store of such things, improving their daily lives as a result, but breaking up the notion of neighbourliness as we all closed our previously open doors and sat in front of our television sets, or 'idiots' lanterns' as my Physics master called them.

* * *

As an aside, and to illustrate how open people's houses were, most doors in the street had the same kind of original lock on the front doors and most of them had a length of string tied to the latch which passed across the back of the letterbox. By pushing open any

Coronation of Queen Elizabeth II

letterbox in the street, anyone could pull on the string and the front door would unlock.

That's how we all liked it: so that whilst eating, for example, we often had someone just appear in the room for some reason or other. When it was warm in summer, front doors were left wide open everywhere in the street, summers seeming so much warmer and sunnier then, which is probably wrong; but they were so warm that leaving the front door open was a necessity in order to cool the house. Ours also had a pale green canvas curtain suspended in the porch to keep the sun off the front door.

We lived with our grandparents who, when my brother was born, moved from the main living room (which we called the kitchen) into the smaller 'middle room'. Each evening, after dinner, they would habitually come into the living room for an evening in front of the television. We'd turn around two chairs for them which backed up against the table, and we'd all watch the glowing screen for the evening.

The same habits were taking place up and down the street, until even on pleasant summer evenings, few people were outside as they used to be, talking and chatting to their neighbours. On summer evenings before television, Grange Gardens, for example, would be packed with people, chatting and strolling, the children playing and old folks sucking on ice creams. Sometimes a band would play and deck chairs would be set out in large numbers.

135

Cars too were changing. Going were designs based on the idea that it was a self-propelled carriage. Coming were shapes and designs which saw the car as a vehicle with a character all its own. One of the very first ones to show this innovation was the Morris Minor, although the little Morris Eight before it had some similar features. It was certainly the first car I saw to have headlights built into the bodywork and not to have separate mudguards and running boards. Its doors were also hinged from the front for safety

Morris Minor

I was in junior school when this car was first produced. One of the teachers had bought one and the whole of our class was taken outside to look at it because it was so different and it was coloured pale green! Previously cars were nearly always dark in colour – black mostly, but also maroon, dark green and, as John W next door had, a lovely dark blue.

Dad began his car-owning career with a tiny, black Austin Seven. This still had mudguards, as did the horse-drawn carriages of old. It had a cloth roof too and the engine was accessed by lifting one half of the bonnet which had a long hinge down the top and centre of it.

A tiny 500 cc engine powered the car. It had no water pump, relying on convection to get the cooling water flowing. It had no oil pump either and used what was known as the 'spit and hope' lubrication system.

The reason I know all this is that when I was about twenty I bought an old Austin Seven for £15 and rebuilt it. It gave me a fine grounding in how cars worked – or didn't – and also some experience of how difficult these old cars were to drive. A particular incident springs to mind which illustrates this.

I had driven to see my now wife in Ystalyfera and was returning down the hill known as the Tumble, west of Cardiff. It was (and is) a fairly steep hill but, more importantly, it was a long one. As I drove the car down it, I tried to change from top to third gear and in doing so the gear lever snapped off. So now the car was stuck in top gear and I couldn't use the gears to slow it down. So I stepped on the

Austin Seven

footbrake, harder and harder and realised that the brakes had become so hot they were no longer working.

On the floor of the car, in front of the accelerator, was a brass disc, about 6 inches in diameter. In order to tighten the brakes, which were activated not hydraulically but by wires, I had to slide this disc to one side and bend down and turn a knob which tightened these wires or cables. Luckily I managed to do this and steer at the same time, but the car was still careering down the hill at an increasing speed.

Seeing the bend at the bottom, I managed to steer the car round it, tyres squealing. Luckily no one else was on the road and I was able to slow down sufficiently by zig zagging across the whole width of the road to reduce speed, before entering Cardiff's Ely district. I finally brought the car to a halt by allowing the tyres to rub the curb and mount the pavement onto some grass. I pulled over and allowed the brakes (and my forehead) to cool down before limping home in top gear to repair the snapped gear lever.

This sort of thing was not that unusual for drivers to have to cope with, together with engines which often caught fire (Dad was a hero once for putting out such a fire with a water-filled pump-action fire extinguisher which he always carried). Tyres would burst; brakes fail, even wheels come off because the king pins snapped, something I witnessed several times. All in a day's driving.

The new cars were gradually putting these dangerous problems behind us and innovations such as rack-and-pinion steering meant that driving was becoming a lot safer and more enjoyable. Lights were brighter, brakes got better, direction indicators and rear stop lights were introduced, even radios were available in cars, albeit valve radios.

Some earlier cars had direction indicators but they were really difficult to see and quite amusing in their own way. Glowing yellow arms, about 8 inches long, would appear from within the door pillars on one side or another, according to which the direction the driver intended moving. Being normally hidden within the door post, a relay would pull them up into position. But the leverage was poor and the hinges often stuck with rust so that drivers were never sure if the indicator had popped out or not.

Dad was often seen, to our amusement, banging furiously on the door post of the Ford (the Austin didn't have indicators at all and hand signals had to be used) in order to bring the indicator to life. Then it would slowly rise and sometimes even get stuck in the 'up' position. Then he'd have to wind down his window and pull it down. But his window-winder on the Ford had packed up, so he had to raise the window by hand and jam it shut with cardboard as well. There was never a dull moment driving.

In general, the new non-repairable goods were seen as a good thing, but many people, my grandfather included, forecast the beginning of a bad trend.

Previously all things, whether they were shoes or wirelesses, were made to last and to be repaired. Now, these new goods could not be repaired, or if they were, the cost was high. Consumerism had arrived. With it, repair businesses gradually collapsed: cobblers, bike repair shops (there were three in Grangetown alone), bespoke tailoring, umbrella men, all went out of business. Yes, there were even men who came around the streets to repair your umbrella, sharpen your knives and fix your pots and pans. All these disappeared.

These were very individual and valuable service industries; valuable in the sense that they provided a door-to-door service for people. In fact everything was brought to your door in those days. Groceries were delivered free; newspapers too of course and milk; soft drinks (the Corona man); and even salt and vinegar.

The latter was delivered on the back of a horse-drawn cart, in huge blocks with vinegar in wooden casks. People came out with a bowl, and the salt and vinegar man cut a lump off the blocks of salt with a very rusty saw and popped it into your bowl. Once in the kitchen, we had to get rid of the rust, of course. Similarly with vinegar, he'd draw off whatever volume your bottle contained from the casks. Simple! It needed no packaging, was a doorstep service and was cheap.

The advent of consumerism, driven basically by larger profit margins from large-volume production runs, meant the advent of pre-packed food and other goods which hadn't been packed before.

Knife Grinder

Butter, for example, sugar, biscuits, bread, all these things had been obtained at the local grocer's and served there and then in whatever volume or weight you wished or could afford, directly into your bag or basket, wrapped in paper if necessary. If you had a large order, the grocer's boy would ride on his delivery bike to your house with your order.

Suddenly, we were being forced into buying things in quantities and volumes decided by someone else, the producer, for his convenience, not ours. Worse, the packaging no one had needed before had to be just thrown away. Many felt this to be wrong, even immoral, forcing on them a restriction in choice. The new consumerism was beginning to have an ugly face. We may not have needed a full half-pound of butter, but that's all the manufacturers would provide, take it or leave it (or, worse, throw away any that was unused).

I came across a quotation some years ago by a Mr Victor Lebow, an American economic advisor to the US Government, showing that consumerism was a very deliberate policy on behalf of governments as well as industry:

> "Our enormously productive economy now demands that we convert the buying and use of goods and services into rituals, that we seek our spiritual satisfaction - our ego satisfaction - from consumption. We need things to be consumed, used up, not to last; to be burned up, worn out, discarded and at an ever-increasing rate."

October 1944 - note the early date

I have always been shocked at the immorality bound up in these words. This idea had little or nothing to do with simple efficiency; it was deliberately introducing waste and squander on a global scale. Of course it filtered down to the lowest and most local levels and we saw its effects in Grangetown as elsewhere.

I remember that it came as a shock to my grandparents and my grandfather was particularly vocal about it. He felt strongly that this attitude to buying, consuming and then throwing things away, would bring disaster. It was easy then to scoff at his words, but how right he was. (We apparently throw away 30% of food world-wide.)

He was brought up with a morality which viewed waste as 'sinful', to be avoided as a question of principle. His generation was proud of the way they could make things go round: being frugal was a way of life. For example, we used to save up all the last bits of soap in the house, dissolve them and evaporate them down to make a larger block; candle wax similarly.

Most goods were made to last in his time; there should be no need to keep replacing things. In the 40s and 50s this attitude was still very prevalent. My grandfather used to keep his tools wrapped in oiled paper to prevent them rusting. He bought a saw *once* and kept it all his life. He had a handful of paint brushes which he also had for a long time, washing them and keeping them wrapped for the next time they were needed. In my own case, once I was eleven, I had my first full-sized bicycle (as a reward for passing the eleven-plus exam) and this was meant to last my lifetime, as my grandfather's had and actually did.

Grocery shop

The first supermarket I came across was a shop called Bateman's, in Corporation Road. This was not a shop as I'd always known one. Normally, a grocer, for example, would stand behind his counter, the stacked shelves surrounding the inside of the shop, and get each item for you, whatever you wanted in whatever quantity you wanted. In this new kind of shop, there was no counter. The customer had to find what he or she wanted themselves, load

Police panda car

up a basket and take everything to a till at the doorway. The idea of service had been abandoned and the customer had to do most of the work.

Goods, in crude piles, large boxes, or sacks, were piled up everywhere. There was no cosy, orderly atmosphere and the people on the till (cash desk) seemed not to worry whether they stocked what you wanted, they were more interested in the time it took for you to pay and leave. Turnover and volume were now king, not service.

Even the comforting and helpful bus conductors were going and passengers were effectively abandoned to fend for themselves when getting on a bus with luggage or needing advice as to the route to take.

The same change, away from genuine customer service and comfort and towards profitability and volume sales could be seen being introduced in transport. Going were the friendly conductors, the helpful porters at stations, the restaurant cars on trains and the space and comfort on aeroplanes. In-coming was price competition, slimmed-down services and poorer quality goods which lasted just a few years and no more. It all smacked of a loss of pride and of a sense of value of both goods and services. Those companies that continued to try and make quality products, or continued to provide conductors on buses, couldn't compete and went broke.

For reasons that none of us could understand, all the valuable and comforting aspects of goods and services were suddenly unaffordable. Even policemen disappeared from our streets and were squeezed into 'Panda' cars. I've never known why these patrol cars were called this.

So the 60s and onwards were periods of great, and sometimes alarming, change; what was happening to us was totally out of our control and dictated by very large (and growing) global industries. Gone were the small, local businesses: shops in our area closed at an ever-increasing rate; transport became poor; the train network was slashed by over 60% by Lord Beeching in 1963 and life seemed out of

Wartime bus conductress

control, changes were being driven not by us, the people, but by big business.

We were acquiring more and more material things, but neighbourliness, a sense of duty and mutual respect, faith in the police and the educational system, political trust, quality – all were in steep decline compared with the late 40s and early 50s. In many ways I feel our country has never really recovered its pride or optimism.

This period certainly saw the UK as a failing manufacturer, mainly because it couldn't bring itself to innovate and change as quickly as those nations that had been heavily bombed and their economies destroyed during the war. They rebuilt everything from scratch, using our money, which made a crippling burden for us. Our industries were comparatively intact, our trade routes covered the whole globe and in principle we had it made. But we failed to notice what was going on in countries like Japan and Germany in particular. Perhaps we'd had enough of making an effort. The country was tired.

The famous motorbikes we used to produce, such as BSA, Norton, Triumph, etc are often quoted as classic examples of how to go broke. They were the world's finest bikes at the time, so much so, their makers saw no need to change them. Once Japanese and German industries were rebuilt (partly with our taxes), they had the opportunity to think afresh, from basics, as to how such machines should be. We didn't have that luxury or the huge capital required. Britain had won the war and yet it was we who rebuilt the economies of Germany and France.

It was a British officer who insisted the VW plant be preserved and put back into production. We had no massive injection of capital like they did. So it wasn't until the 1980s after much industrial unrest, that the country realised it had to sweep aside large sections of its ailing industries and make a fresh start.

One of the main reasons we as a young family decided to go and live in Switzerland was because of the effects of these changes, which caused great social unrest and strife. In 1973, the country was on its knees due to strikes. It was functioning for only three days a week; each area of the country was allowed to work for three selected days only, to save on electricity because the miners had gone on strike. Our homes and offices were in darkness the rest of the time, and we lived by candlelight and cooked on camping stoves. Transport was severely curtailed too, so we couldn't get around. Petrol was effectively rationed and food was scarce. Inflation hit 23% and the higher rate of income tax was 98%! Rubbish was piled high in the streets because other unions came out on strike in sympathy with the miners. It was even impossible to bury the dead.

This was the crunch: the Prime Minister, Edward Heath, resigned because the country had become ungovernable. The country had to choose between being held to ransom by the unions, who saw their jobs being cut as we lost markets all over the world, and voting in a government that would shake up the country and sort out the mess. They voted for Mrs Thatcher. Meanwhile, we as a family were very glad we had escaped to Switzerland and France and were enjoying a much better quality of life, safe from the anarchy of the unions.

CHAPTER TWELVE
Fancy Some Tripe?

I doubt whether we would contemplate now eating much of what we ate in the 40s and 50s. I have witnessed many instances recently where meat, for example, that is pre-packed and devoid of all fat, is seen as the standard by which butchers' produce should be judged. Whereas in the post-war decades, meat was seen for what it is: the bodies of animals; and animal meat is not all naturally beautifully pink and fat-free. More to the point, it does not naturally occur wrapped in cling film in a polystyrene tray either.

In the 40s and 50s, a visit to Cardiff Market would be an entirely different experience to nowadays. Whole carcasses hung from hooks, rabbits and other wild animals such as pheasants and pigeons also hung there, complete with plumage, all dripping blood onto the sawdust covered floor.

At Christmas, we had to pluck and gut the chicken ourselves. A butcher would do this for a fee, but most people did it themselves. Blood, guts or offal were evident everywhere. The heads of animals were not only evident, but were purchased for meals, a pig's head being particularly popular, as was its organs.

My grandmother was a particular lover of offal. Most weeks, she would boil tripe (intestines) in dilute milk in a large, black saucepan with a very long handle, over the living room fire. It needed a protracted cooking time to make it tender, but it was completely free of fat and provided excellent, cheap protein. These days, such food is probably incorporated into animal food, which, when you think about it, is a waste.

Plate of cooked tripe

DOCTORS RECOMMEND IT.

TRIPE *It's Good for You.* **TRIPE**

Pioneers of the Tripe Trade

Cooked in Cardiff

'Phone 760.

35, ALBANY ROAD
209, COWBRIDGE ROAD.
92, CITY ROAD.
90, CORNWALL STREET.

EXCEL PRODUCTS CO.,
2, CHURCH STREET, CARDIFF.

Tripe advertisement

Cooked pig's head

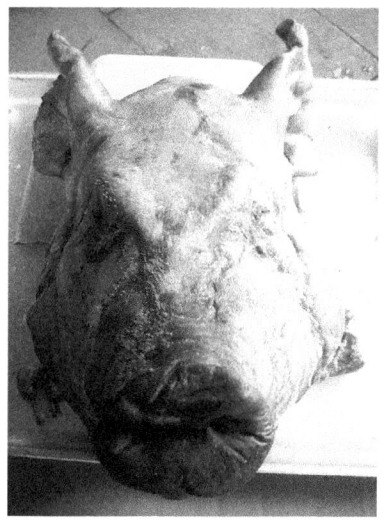

Back then, tripe was claimed not only to be good for you but was allegedly recommended by doctors.

She would also buy rabbits, whole ones, complete with head and fur, which she would skin and gut herself. We were viscerally aware of where our meat came from and didn't shy away from dealing with the bodies of animals. Chickens, kept in back yards, had to be slaughtered, plucked and gutted and this was an everyday experience.

Just as we faced up to other realities in life, such as the preparing of the body of a deceased relative for burial, so we had no illusions about where our food came from. This is in stark contrast to today, when many people don't seem to realise where their food comes from or how it comes to them, hygienically wrapped, the back-room operations hidden.

Offal these days is bought by very few people, the majority considering it an unacceptable food; food that should not be seen because of its origins and functions. I suppose the argument is that kidneys that produce urine or tripe that produce faeces are offensive; but that is actually pretty silly and results in a huge amount of wasted protein.

During and after the war, offal was one of the staple meats on the table and this continued well into the early 60s. Butchers' shops exposed all the parts of animals for everyone to see. Shoppers were well versed in the various cuts of meat, the functions of organs and ways of cooking them. It was a delicacy to have an entire pig's head on the table and there were often mild arguments over who should have the best parts, such as the cheeks.

Perhaps today's consumer would be shocked to see a butcher's shop of that era. Sawdust covered the floor to absorb the blood that dripped from carcasses of various animals that were hung for weeks to improve flavour. Buckets of tripe, blood, liver, kidneys and other offal were on show alongside unaffordable delicacies such as lamb; for lamb occurred only during the spring when male lambs are slaughtered and was a luxury. Otherwise, we ate the bodies of old ewes, sold as mutton. The notion of killing young lambs was not embraced; better to slaughter old, worn-out ewes that were at the end of their lives.

Many ingenious recipes were used to make offal, which is generally tasteless, more palatable. Sausages, faggots, pasties and pies were all popular methods of producing cheap but nourishing meals. Of course, this meant work; little or nothing of this sort of food was pre-prepared, although most butchers sold sausages, black pudding made with blood, and faggots. In fact, in most markets, one could usually find a stall or two that specialised in meals of sausages or faggots.

Faggots and peas in a bowl with rich gravy was a cheap and nourishing meal when out shopping. Cardiff Market provided a choice of such establishments and the smell of the food cooking was a big draw. Sometimes added value in the form of chips would also be available.

Cardiff once had a thriving fishing fleet, although modest compared with those in the north-east of England, of course. But it ensured that fresh fish could be had, often from the dockside.

One large store that provided excellent cheap lunches was Woolworths, on Queen Street. At the back of the large shop was a kitchen and restaurant area, the walls and counters covered in white tiles. One sat to eat at a curved, tiled and rather high counter, sitting on high, rotating stools, which were always a source of amusement for children as they practiced spinning around on them. Even without sitting on one, if the seat itself were spun fast enough, it felt as though it would almost take off! The menu majored on pies, pasties, faggots and peas, fish and chips. Yum!

Perhaps one of the reasons we were all so much healthier and slimmer then, was that we did not indulge in poor quality food, food with more calories than was necessary; although men who had tough labouring jobs needed a carbohydrate-rich and protein-rich diet. Mothers and wives made sure the men received the best nourishment in the family, because if they became too weak to work, the family would suffer.

We had very few sweets, or delicacies. Cakes we had, but only when the ingredients were available and affordable. Butter, for example and sugar, were expensive and were rationed until I was eleven. Our allowance of meat, eggs, bread and milk was very modest during the war and after it, until rationing stopped. Although meals often left us feeling a little hungry, it was one of the best diets to have followed. Even today, my generation sees many modern tastes in food as wasteful and unhealthy.

The introduction of pre-wrapped and pre-weighed foods was seen as wasteful and as preventing us from exercising choice and frugality. Once manufacturers became the ones deciding the basic units of food we used, food waste shot up and the packaging created waste that had not existed previously.

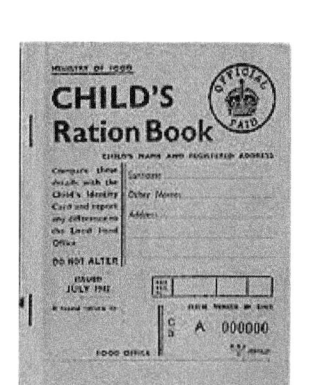

All the items we took home after shopping were either wrapped in greaseproof paper, such as cheese and meat, or in newspaper or, sometimes, brown paper. These, except for the wrapping on meat, were often reused in the home. Newspapers were used to light the fire or as toilet paper; string was salvaged and the brown paper reused to wrap parcels, tied with string and sealed with sealing wax. The weekly meat ration was particularly small, at 4 ounces or 226 grams. The allowance of processed meats such as ham and bacon were half that. Here is a list of other weekly foods:

- Butter and cheese - 2 oz each or 56 g
- Margarine - 4 oz
- Cooking fat - 4 oz
- Milk - 3 pints
- Sugar - half a pound
- Preserves - half a pound a month
- Tea - 2 oz a week
- Eggs - 1 a week
- Sweets - 12 oz a month

Child's Ration Book

Child's Identity Card

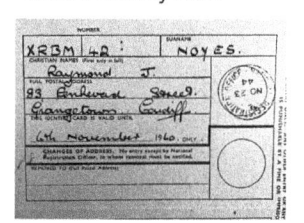

We had to present a book of ration tokens to shopkeepers to withdraw these amounts, books that were as precious as gold. Queues were always long and much patience was needed. But since everyone was in the same boat, the only pragmatic way of coping was to be tolerant and most people were.

We children had our own ration books. It was forbidden to swap tokens (each token had a colour and was labelled as to the food to which it applied) but it was allowed to swap the food once withdrawn. Quite a vigorous trade in food therefore occurred, with we children used as runners between houses and streets. Someone who didn't like so much milk would swap it for sugar, or flour, perhaps. We runners often crossed paths and exchanged information as to whose house we were going to and what we were swapping. Although the rationing of food is probably the strongest impression, perhaps because hunger is a very basic memory, clothing, shoes, petrol and all sorts of other essentials were also rationed.

Other official documents that had to be guarded carefully included identity cards and I still have mine, which was valid until 1960.

I think a particular feature of our food during rationing and into the early 60s was its fat content. For example, chips were usually fried in lard, which was bought in great slabs; on Mondays after a beef Sunday lunch, the fat that had dripped off the meat into the roasting tray would be spread, as it was, onto toast for breakfast. We usually ate butter rather than margarine, if the budget allowed it. Margarine was seen as a very inferior and rather tasteless substitute for butter and my mother used to apologise to visitors if she had to serve them margarine.

Meats such as mutton, which are fairly rich in fat, would be cleaned off the bone at a meal and the bones either sucked for their bone marrow or boiled up for a stew. If a family kept a dog, it may have been given the bone at the end of this process. Pets ate what we ate.

It is amusing to step back a little in order to realise just how much the language and knowledge of food has changed as we have innovated and expanded our diet, adopting that of other countries. Our diet is now very eclectic. When I was growing up, a takeaway was arithmetic, pasta and pizza were unknown, bananas were only seen at Christmas and a Big Mac was a large raincoat.

Once rationing was over, we who were raised during the war saw for the first time exotic foods such as bananas and oranges. Having been used to bland food, the smell of them was really strong and some came wrapped in tissue paper, which could be used to replace newspaper in the lavatory. At Christmas, our stockings would always contain a tangerine because it was so exotic and

Queuing during rationing

Royal Arcade, Cardiff

rare. To this day, the smell of a tangerine evokes Christmas mornings.

As imports became affordable and we became hungry for some minor luxuries, we saw tinned food as an opportunity to indulge ourselves, notably on Sundays. Sunday afternoons often saw the opening of a tin of salmon (amongst four people) or a tin of fruit, such as pears or peaches. This would be eaten with lots of bread and butter, to fill out the meal, and often with a small tin of condensed milk. Condensed milk is what it says on the tin: about a third of the water content is removed, so that it resembles watery cream. Such Sunday teas were quite a treat and were standard fare when visitors came or we visited someone else. Sunday afternoons were often spent visiting friends and relatives.

Sunday lunch was the main family meal of the week, when everyone would be together, and after rationing it was usually fairly sumptuous. But it was the only occasion on which a joint of meat was cooked. The leftovers were used for at least two days afterwards, Mondays being 'fry-up' day for the cold meat, potatoes and greens and Tuesdays was a broth made from the bones together with boiled potatoes.

Keeping food fresh could be a problem, but bearing in mind that shops were everywhere within easy walking distance, we could buy fresh food daily anyway. Any leftovers would be stored in what was called a safe. This was a small metal cabinet with air holes in it here and there, covered in fine mesh to keep out flies. Such safes were kept in the coolest part of the kitchen, which was the pantry. Most houses in our area had one.

Pantries were effectively a small, walk-in cupboard, containing a large slab of either marble or stone which remained cool, connected as it was to the walls of the little room. Butter, cheese, bacon and milk were kept on this slab, usually on plates and covered with pottery to keep them cool. If the weather was really warm, the pottery would be wetted to cool it. The pantry was ventilated from the outside, and had no windows, usually, so if it was north-facing, it kept fairly cool.

I have to admit that the pantry was one of my favourite parts of the house. It often contained a cake, a tart or fruit, so a lightning raid on the pantry when no one was looking could be rewarding.

Pantries also contained drinks. In ours, ginger beer was usually brewing, a drink for which my grandmother, for some reason, had become the chief brewer. Eventually, soft drinks were again available, delivered to the front door by companies such as Corona or Tizer. My favourite was dandelion and burdock, its dark brown colour imitating Guinness.

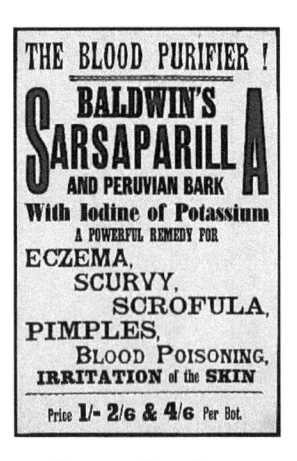

There were other more unusual drinks made or sold, such as sarsaparilla. This herbal drink, based on the root of the exotic sarsaparilla plant from South America, was introduced from the States, a legacy of the temperance movement. Some manufacturers made exaggerated claims that it could cure almost anything.

Sarsaparilla advert

There was a sarsaparilla 'bar' in the Royal Arcade where the drink was served on draft from small versions of beer pumps. My father often took me there, as though we men were sharing a drink in a pub. Good male bonding stuff! Unfortunately, when it closed, the owner or brewer did not pass on his or her secret recipe, which was a pity.

The rationing of food also had benefits. Babies and pregnant mothers had special allowances of lovely things such as concentrated orange juice. It was a very sugary concentrate, meant to be heavily diluted with water. Undiluted, straight from the bottle, it was fabulous!

This led to my downfall. One day, my mother had just had a fresh allowance of several bottles of this lovely drink destined for my young brother. She stored in the safe in the conservatory, which was attached to the 'middle room' where we then lived. I thought it would be a great idea to invite a number of friends to a mock party in the back yard, the centrepiece of which would be this concentrated orange juice.

Mam was out at the time and we drank almost all of it. Needless to say I had a good row when Dad came home and I don't think I have liked orange juice as much since, although none has tasted so good.

Sweets were available commercially and there were some splendid sweet shops around, dispensing loose sweets of all imaginable types, tastes and colours from large glass jars that were arranged by the dozen on shelves. However, many households made their own, especially toffee, which is pretty simple. Most houses had a toffee hammer with which to break up a tray of it. The commercially made ones were, however, our firm favourites because of the sheer variety and colours.

Sherbet was also very popular, often bought with a stick of liquorice which was dipped into it and sucked. The sherbet was taken from a large jar using a small steel shovel and weighed out onto paper which was cleverly made into a cone by the shopkeeper.

Some bottles of sherbet were very attractive, because occasionally several colours would be contained in the one jar. I think that on the whole, my favourite form of liquorice was the wheel. It was a fairly soft liquorice and because it was compact, it was handy to have in a schoolboy's pocket, picking up fluff and all manner of pocket detritus as it rested there.

The inventiveness of the industry was to be applauded with sweets such as gobstoppers. These quite large balls had multiple layers of different colours in them and they lasted a very long time. It was only when the ball had been sucked to a size small enough to be bitten, that one could eventually demolish the thing. Attempting to crack open the so-called 'jawbreaker' gobstopper too early broke many a tooth.

It was unwise to try sucking a gobstopper in school, not only because it would prevent one from speaking (stopping the gob!) but it often left tell-tale colours on the lips and fingers. I have no idea what dyes were used in their preparation, but they were quite tenacious and would take some time to wash off the face or hands. Sticky fingers that contaminated an exercise book would be left stinging by a teacher before the offender was sent to wash his or her hands.

Girls were much better than boys at keeping clean and tidy and managed to avoid sweet stains. They usually carried a handkerchief which helped, sucking it to help remove the dirt. They also used them to make animal shapes, such as a rabbit. They seemed to be

Bottles of concentrated orange juice for infants

always playing with their handkerchiefs, whereas we boys tended to use our clothes as a means of cleaning anything, including our noses!

Handkerchiefs were things that everyone just had to have; they were one of the most popular gifts at Christmas or birthdays. Men often had a silk handkerchief in their top pockets when dressing to go out. Women tucked dainty versions, often elaborately made, into bracelets. So valued were they as a must-have item that the larger department stores would have a department that specialised in them, the store's Handkerchief and Scarves Department.

CHAPTER THIRTEEN
Oh, the Hokey-Kokey!

A feature of life on our island in the city was the natural cadences into which time was organised: the peace and rest of Sundays being the most marked. The year also had its punctuation marks: all the Christian festivals were celebrated as was the monarch's birthday, Armistice Day and so on.

Bank holidays were very special and were used as a valuable opportunity for family amusement and recreation, not a period for shopping because the shops were all closed, including our local ones. Many men, especially, worked as much overtime as they could to boost the family income, so a bank holiday was particularly valued.

Christian festivals were religious occasions and non-commercial. An air of genuine celebration pervaded households during these periods. Even if one was not religious, these festivals had a clear, reverent and special feel about them.

The emphasis at Christmas, for example, was not so much on buying presents, but of celebrating the significance of the religious occasion: by carol singing, going to church and to concerts (notably to hear Handel's *Messiah*) and getting together in family groups or with one's immediate neighbours.

It was a time given over to thinking of others; not only the family, but also neighbours and friends. It was certainly a time for giving, often of presents that one had made oneself. Most of the decorations in the house were made ourselves too. My mother's knitting always moved up a gear before Christmas.

In our house, we would of course have the familiar tree and decorations as well as Christmas lunch and all the rest, but it would be a period when social things were done. We would invite neighbours and friends to come and have a drink, sing some songs together, accompanied by my father on the piano or on the accordion. People would come and recite something, play an instrument or we'd all play parlour games, cards, tell jokes and generally make merry.

Of course Christmas did involve the purchase of a few presents but, except for children, they were often fairly simple and modest. Presents for fathers, for example, may have consisted of a pair of socks or perhaps handkerchiefs. The gesture was the most important aspect, although I can remember my father anticipating yet another pair of unexciting socks as he opened his presents! Mothers tended to get scented talcum powder, bath salts or bath soap, as though to hint that they all needed a good bath.

As for special food and drink at Christmas, it was pretty well the only time when alcohol was drunk in the house; sherry, brandy and beer being the favourites; but no wine, which was difficult to get and beyond our reach both economically and culturally. Although we did have a bottle of white wine once with our Christmas chicken, sweet Sauterne, a dessert wine, which was totally inappropriate really but was an exciting extra to the meal. We always had chicken for Christmas lunch, turkey being too expensive.

Christmas was the only period in the year when mandarin oranges and dates were available. Dad would always buy a cigar or two and the fire would be lit in the front room, which was a rarity. So my memories of Christmas are olfactory ones of cigar smoke, old out-of-date sherry, Christmas lunch and mandarin oranges, besides the magical glow of the lights on the tree and the decorations.

My memories are also auditory: carol singing by children at the front door and by choirs in the street; the Salvation Army's brass band; fog horns, ships' hooters and dancing.

Before Christmas Day, we kids would go carol singing, usually in a small group of two or three singers, otherwise the takings were too meagre. In addition, we roped in younger brothers or sisters because they would be thrust to the front and told to look poor and cold.

We usually did quite well; earning enough for a spending spree at the sweet shop, where large jars of our favourite sweets would line the shelves. My favourites were Jelly Babies, Pear Drops (which would give you a good 'trip' if you ate too many), Gob Stoppers, barley sugar and various liquorices, some of natural root (so-called

Spanish Root) and others made into shapes: pipes with 'hundreds and thousands' on their bowls, shoe laces, and liquorice rolls.

There was a newsagents at the top of our street where the proprietor's mother made toffee. She'd come out from the back room-cum-kitchen with a warm tray of it and break it up in front of us with a small hammer. Fresh toffee is lovely, especially when still warm. Our earnings at carol singing would make this affordable too.

There was quite a lot of competition for carol singing. In our own house we sometimes used to get fed up with the number of carol singers calling, so I expect it was the same for our customers too, although we rarely got chased away and were almost always given a few pennies.

Besides the amateurs like us, we also had competition from professionals, because Christmas was always marked by open-air recitals by the 'Sally Army' brass band. These were really excellent players and the sound they made was wonderfully round and deep.

It filled the street with a lovely warm sound. We would sometimes follow them as they walked to their next patch. The women Army members would knock on doors and make a collection.

Preaching by the Salvation Army

In a similar spirit, those of us who went to church or chapel would take the opportunity of putting as much money in the charity box as possible. This was what our Christmases were about: charity and neighbourliness, not (yet) things.

As now, Christmas needed organising and my mother was the organiser. She would begin the preparations by making a Christmas cake, one that was of course rich and somewhat alcoholic and which matured in the cool pantry. She was quite good at icing them, a procedure I always observed, mainly in order to pick up any waste icing and even, if my luck was in, marzipan.

Nearer the great day, mince pies were produced in large numbers, although keeping them fresh was a problem, so she had to keep cooking batches of them as the days were ticked off. I suppose if my brother and I hadn't been so intent on diminishing their numbers by raiding the pantry she wouldn't have had to keep making so many.

On Christmas Day, it seemed that Mam was rarely seen, as she worked in the kitchen and brought in more and more food. Although her excuse for spending most of her time out there was that there was a lot to do, I think the real reason was that she didn't like the noise and general mayhem to be found in the front room. The men tended to be those making the most noise, having loosened up their vocal chords with sufficient bottles of stout, never, of course drunk out of the bottle. The women on the other hand would usually flock together in the kitchen, ensuring that the semi-industrial assembly line of sandwich-making was kept moving.

We had a couple of friends, A and M, who would come with their families, the former being an inveterate story-teller, even if we'd heard them all before. He had a very strident voice, so you just had to listen to him.

My grandfather would play the spoons and the saw. I don't know how or when he practiced these arts, but I remember being mesmerized the first time he did it. He played the saw with the bow from my mother's violin. She used to play very occasionally, but I never remember her doing so at a party.

Playing the spoons was amusing. They were just a pair of dessert spoons taken between the fingers and tapped energetically on various hard parts of the body, of which the knees were favourite. They also produced a suitable tinkle on the thighs, the soles of the shoes and when running up and down the forearms. Quite funny to watch! As for the sound from the saw, it was actually rather weird, because being bent at different angles of curvature in order to obtain different notes, the sound was not constant, the player introducing a degree of vibrato into his performance, producing a spooky sound as though a ghost were about to appear.

Dancing was also a feature of these get-togethers, although it always caused Dad some concern as he witnessed his piano rocking back and fore as the floor bent rhythmically under the load. Elsie H was the instigator and self-styled teacher of dancing (not to mention her romantic match-making schemes) at these events. Her two daughters, P and J were recruited to persuade my brother and me and to become romantic and dance with them. We didn't always manage to refuse and we therefore experienced our first lessons in dancing at the hands of these 'fanatics', albeit we only did the waltz and fox trot.

We tried the Gay Gordons and other Scottish specialties once, but the floor wouldn't take it and we had to stop. We quickly realised that several people jumping up and down on the floor simultaneously could accelerate its end; we had to break up our step as soldiers do when crossing a weak bridge. It was also a good excuse to stop our enforced romancing.

Dancing wasn't restricted to the house; we also danced in the street on New Year's Eve. Neighbours flooded out into the street, drinks in hand, to do the 'Hokey Cokey' in a large circle the diameter of which reached from pavement to pavement. On one occasion, when the weather was fine, Dad was persuaded to go and get his accordion and we danced the Gay Gordons and the Conga, the latter leading in and out of various houses for what seemed like hours.

Once Christmas Day was behind us, the rest of the period was full of parties and many were held in our house. We wouldn't always be the family to invite everyone round, but we were one of the few houses with both a piano and a good pianist under the same roof; so we tended to be the focal point at our end of the street. One of our next door neighbours was a lovely Jamaican couple and the wife could sing really well, so she would entertain everyone. Her favourite song was Mary's Boychild, Jesus Christ. My grandmother bought the music for me so that I could accompany the singer, to my great embarrassment.

I was to be further embarrassed one Christmas when someone, as yet still unknown, volunteered me to play *Silent Night* on the piano at the evening chapel service. I love the piano, but at, say, seven years of age, one is not necessarily enamoured of public performances when hardly being able to reach the pedals and the piece is in the key of D-flat.

Then there were the so-called 'uncles', who were really friends of my parents or simply neighbours. Some would bring a guitar or other instrument. They would drop in during the daytime and have a jazz session with Dad. He also played the accordion; it would be brought out of mothballs and he'd lead a sing-song of an evening, with the front room packed and rocking on its weak floorboards.

Cardiff city centre was not as illuminated as it is now. The centre of attraction was always the large Norwegian Spruce Christmas tree, an annual gift from Norway for our sacrifice in liberating them from the Germans. The erection of the tree in front of the City Hall, accompanied by bands and choirs was a lovely event to which we often went. These days the tree tends to be either in the shopping centre or in front of the castle.

Trolley buses, being electric, were lit up, on their electric collector arms, but the main attraction in town for children was Howells' and David Morgans' Christmas toy fairs. These department stores used to compete for putting on the best show. I was always a fan of Howells because most years they not only had the usual Santa's Grotto, but also a huge (and I mean huge) electric train set.

Train and Meccano sets were very popular then. So I often used to pick my desired present from amongst the latest 'Hornby Dublo' train sets. 'Triang' also made trains sets and my school friend Robert C had one, but they were made of new-fangled plastic, whereas Hornby still made their rolling stock of die-cast metal. The only negative thing about Hornby, which used to give those friends of mine who had Triang trains the edge, was that Hornby used three rails on their track, the centre one being the live rail whereas theirs was more realistic with two. But I still preferred my heavy, metal engines with their greater detail, my pride and joy being a model of The Duchess of Athol.

Uncle A and his two boys, B and G, had the best train set on the street. Adrian S, directly across the street from us also had a set, but smaller than mine. Uncle A, being a carpenter, went to town on the construction of his train set and even knocked a hole in the wall from their middle room into the living room, so that the train set could travel around the house. He built shelving around two rooms and alpine scenery through which the trains would pass. He spent a lot of time making what was an amazing set-up. I admit to being jealous.

Our train set was erected temporarily in what was then our 'box room' on a sheet of rather bendy hardboard, supported on a metal frame, so it wasn't a permanent fixture and the trains certainly didn't escape the confines of the small room and travel around the house. But my brother and I, and our friend A from the next street, spent many hours playing with it, making points which changed if we pulled on strings which we attached to them; or we'd put batteries into the carriages with small light bulbs which lit them up. But the batteries were so heavy that the train slowed down quite a lot. It was the beginning of an engineering career.

Cardiff City Hall at Christmas

I remember the year I got that train set. I was very young and was lifted up and put to sit on the sideboard to keep me out of the way. (We had the sideboard in the front room before we had a piano, although we did have my grandmother's organ in there too.) Whilst I was safely out of the way, my father and Uncle A got on with the serious job of setting up the train set for the first time. Mam, I remember, came in and scolded them for depriving me of the fun.

Before the television arrived, we used to listen dutifully to His Majesty King George VI giving his annual Christmas broadcast to the empire, later to become the Commonwealth. In 1952 it became the turn of the new Queen Elizabeth. My grandfather in particular was keen on these annual broadcasts and we all listened attentively. This was serious stuff, because we never heard the monarch on any other occasion. You could tell how important the king or queen were by their accents.

King George was very hesitant in his speech. You had the feeling that he was glad to get to the end of his address because suddenly he stopped stuttering. We should bear in mind that none of these broadcasts were pre-recorded as now. Knowing he was talking live to a third of the globe must have been rather daunting.

***

Easter was, after Christmas, the most important festival of the year. On Good Friday, very few people would work, the shops were closed and Easter Sunday would be one of the very quietest and most solemn days of the year, certainly as quiet as Christmas Day.

First thing in the morning on Good Friday, about 7:30-ish, a baker would make his traditional rounds of Grangetown with his horse and cart, ringing his brass hand bell and shouting, "Hot cross buns, hot cross buns!" and we'd run out (sometimes in pyjamas) and buy them, warm and freshly made that morning. Depending on where he started from, the buns could be hot or just lukewarm when he got to us; but they were a special treat. These delicacies were sold only on that day in the year and only in that special way.

Breakfast on Easter Sunday would be special not only for these unique buns, but for coloured eggs. Of course we had a chocolate Easter egg as a present (usually one), but Mam would boil some ordinary ones for breakfast and add some colouring to the water. Out they'd come pink, or even green. Sometimes, the previous night she'd paint a picture on them in wax from a candle so that a sketch or lettering would stand out from the coloured background.

Other festivals during the year were treated with a similar drive for getting together with others. New Year was a major one and, because it lacked religious significance, we could loosen up a little more. Once we'd heard Big Ben ring out, the fog horns, steel works sirens, hooters of all sorts and especially ship's funnels would welcome the new year. We'd walk out the front door with lumps of coal in order to try and be the first ones to offer good luck with it to our neighbours. This was rapidly followed by singing and dancing up and down the street until the early hours.

Harvest festival was a huge event at our chapel. Bakers would bake bread in the shape of a huge sheaf of wheat. Enormous amounts of fruit and vegetables would be brought by all of us and added to the pile beneath the pulpit.

What a show that was! The smell of fruit and vegetables was striking, perhaps because the chapel normally smelled of wood, varnish and old books so that the change in atmosphere was remarkable. All these gifts would be given to those in Grangetown who were poor and rarely ate fresh fruit and the surplus would go to various Doctor Bernardo's homes for orphans or to the chronically sick at sanatoria.

The best part of this festival was the singing. Sometimes there would be so many people at the service that the main chapel building overflowed into the adjacent hall, which usually served as the scout and cubs hall, but which also had a balcony round it but no pulpit, just a stage. *We plough the fields and scaaaater, the good seed on the land* was always a favourite hymn. It marked another milestone in the year. Even now, when I hear that tune, I feel the seasons are changing but, more importantly, how grateful we should be that the harvest has been good, for us at least.

I've already spoken of Whitsun and the Whitsun Treat. What I haven't mentioned is that in Grangetown was the annual Whitsun walking race, which started and finished at the Catholic Club at the end of our street.

Quite a number of walkers, including my grandfather in one year, used to take part. They set out, numbers pinned to their shirts, at about 9am and had to walk to the top of Leckwith Hill and back, returning around 11am. Banners and bunting were erected across the street and crowds lined the pavements along the route which was about 8 miles or so.

Walking fast requires a strange and exaggerated rolling of the hips and the participants must never break into anything that could be described as a run. To ensure they didn't, many stewards were employed along the route. It's a sport that I haven't seen practiced much and looks exhausting.

Another sport with which Grangetown was associated and continues to be was baseball. Our top team was the Grange Albions. For some reason, baseball took off in Grangetown and it had its own league. One of our relatives, whose name I can't remember, used to be a particularly good player apparently. Two venues hosted baseball: the Marl and Seven Oaks Park, a large green space.

The Marl was, however, a cinder park: just an open field which had been levelled and then compacted with fine, brown cinders or ash. It was fine for running on and we used to play at 'speedway' there on our bikes, but baseball players used to suffer badly grazed arms and legs when playing there. So the preferred location was Seven Oaks Park which was all grass.

It was here that the league games were played. The Albions were very good, so much so that during the war, when an American warship was in dock, the crew challenged them to a game, thinking it would be a push-over, but it wasn't; the Albions won and a number of the team received formal invitations to go and play professionally in the States. As far as I know, none accepted, but their victory was a mark of the standard of the team.

Huge numbers of spectators would gather to watch such matches, whole families picnicking as they watched. It was a really good afternoon's (or evening's) entertainment which was very popular at one time. Just recently I drove past the Marl and noticed that on a pair of gates, an emblematic pair of crossed baseball bats in metal have been fixed to them to remind people of its interesting history.

I should stress that our baseball was not the same spectacle as American baseball. No thrower's mound was involved, for example, but the clothing was similar: long shorts and striped shirts being the most striking features. They didn't wear any face protection either, or baseball caps.

It's interesting and perhaps instructive to note that in days that were free of ready-made entertainment, our days were filled with lots to do. We participated in much more than we do now. We didn't so much go in for pleasure as for enjoyment, which are two very different things. The former requires very little effort, such as sitting in front of the TV, but the latter requires participation, creativity and activity. We certainly seemed very active in the post-war years.

CHAPTER FOURTEEN
Mrs S's Gloves

Each period of history has its icons: its architecture, its fashions, and so on. The 50s had a number of these, not least of all the clothes we wore.

Men's clothes differed little to now, a jacket and trousers being the main structure, as it were; but the detailed styling was slightly different, some elements being inherited from much earlier periods in the 20th century. For example, many older men, such as my grandfather, didn't feel properly dressed unless they wore a waistcoat and for visiting someone he would always wear stiff, starched collars with curved corners.

He always wore a pocket watch and chain: a steel one for work and a gold one for formal wear. He always wore long johns or two-piece woollen underclothes, even in the summer. These covered him from neck to feet, rather like a modern onesie. He often complained of the cold and in the winter he would wear long woollen socks up and beyond his knees. The texture of his long johns (the origin of the name comes from the 19th century heavyweight boxer John L Sullivan who first wore them) used to strike me as particularly odd. They were made, like his working shirts, of coarse wool and must have been particularly itchy to wear.

His working shirts were also collar-less, with holes back and front of the neck into which studs could be passed in order to fix a separate collar. The reason for this is that the collar could then be washed separately to the shirt, the collar becoming dirty quicker. Shirts were washed once a week. Not all his collars were starched white ones, although his Sunday best ones were.

The oil portrait of him below shows him wearing just such a stiff collar. His working collars were of wool and often striped, as if to indicate that this wasn't his best shirt and collar.

John Noyes

He always wore a tie which he tucked into his waistcoat, once he'd wound his pocket watch which he religiously kept accurate to the chimes of Big Ben at 7am every morning. This moment was one he never missed and he always sat briefly in his fireside chair to hear the headline news. You may deduce from these observations that he was a man of habit and routine.

He was a slim man, so he wore his clothes well. His 'best' suit was beautifully cut (handmade, of course) and the material was clearly of good quality. I don't think he had more than two or three such good suits in his lifetime.

The trousers I found interesting, because they were not only slightly tapered but had an elastic tape at the bottom which passed beneath the arch of his shoes to keep them taught – Edwardian style. His best trousers were also without turn-ups. The ensemble was very elegant. With his best gold watch chain, his starched white collar, waistcoat and black polished boots of soft leather, he looked very smart, as did most men at that time. To top it all, he always added a light grey trilby hat. He wore a trilby to work, but of a darker colour.

Of a morning, I would be up as early as he was, watching him make the rounds of household chores which he had adopted as his to perform. It was a special time in the day that just he and I shared. I used to sit on the arm of an armchair adjacent to the table and enjoy the opening of the biscuit barrel containing Bourbon biscuits, my favourite.

Notable amongst his chores was the collecting of coal and wood for the fires in the living room and 'middle' room; after which he would shave and dress for work. When he retired, he also cleaned and polished my shoes and those of my brother for school.

He followed a strict routine and even smoked to the clock; his first Woodbine being after his first cup of morning tea, but he only smoked it half way through, the rest being kept in a waistcoat pocket for the next appointed smoke, often taken outside around 9am.

Even our street lamplighter-upper wore a suit to his work; his was brown. There was little or no industrial clothing then; everyone wore their ordinary clothes and many men went to work at the dirtiest jobs wearing a suit. In summer, they might remove the jacket and work in a waistcoat, even rolling up their sleeves – which was very daring of them.

My grandparents were married in 1908, just outside the Victorian era, but both retained Victorian dress, as evidenced by this wedding painting of my grandmother. They also retained Victorian values.

It may seem odd, but our definition of a formal occasion was quite different to now. Going to town for shopping was a formal occasion and everyone wore their good clothes. It was a matter of pride not to be seen in public in ordinary working clothes. The city centre with its department stores, which were constructed so as to impress, was considered a formal place.

Agnes Noyes

If we look at the Howells department store and examine its architecture we note the Greek columns in stone, the windows and doors in bronze. This was not a building built on the cheap. It was an expensive temple to shopping. Shoppers who approached it, to wander amongst its formal displays of clothes, did not want to be put to shame by a negative comparison with their own. So they wore their best clothes.

Sales counters were constructed in French-polished hardwoods of various kinds, often topped with glass, under which was a vertical pane of glass through which goods on display could be viewed. Generally speaking, if an item was of interest, then the assistant would take one from stock, from multiple drawers arranged along the wall behind the counter. These stock drawers were also of polished wood, some with a small inspection pane of glass in them to make identifying the contents easy.

Department stores and even local haberdasheries selling dress materials were interesting, because the stock they held was often enormous. In particular, the counters on which they were measured and dispensed were unique. Always of polished wood, they would have a brass measure fixed to them (a yard) and some had an automatic measuring machine through which the material had to be pulled to be measured. These shops or departments were, of course, the domains of women. Men had their own in the form of tool shops.

The James Howells Building

One of the most well known in Cardiff was that of John Hall, situated in one of the arcades. Like all such shops, it had a unique smell, one that was not absorbed by soft carpeting or curtains of course but sustained by smooth linoleum underfoot. It seemed something of an Aladdin's Cave. Unlike women's shops, male customers did not engage in tittle-tattle but there was much joking.

The language used in such places was unique. In fact, the language of the tool shop and the DIY specialist remains one that is often felt to be intimidating to women, who do not understand the almost secret and secretive signals being sent by male customers and assistants alike. They speak in code, often only using the dimensions (imperial or metric) they require or the reference number given to the type of fitting they're looking for.

For example, a customer's simple requirement such as buying a length of wood, needs a code, such as 'two-be-one-be-two'. This means 'I want a length of timber two inches by one inch in cross-section and two metres long,' the measures now being a mixture of imperial and metric in the case of timber, which in itself is confusing.

If buying a plumbing fitting it can become even more mysterious: 'a three-quarter Yorkshire male/female forty-five degree reducer' is not some middle-aged hermaphrodite that hails from the north-east of England, but is a copper joint.

This succinct language has to be learned and that is only possible either by being a tradesman or someone who has mastered DIY to a professional level. Having these qualifications means that the men entering John Hall's shop were part of a trade freemasonry, sharing the language of the trades they practiced.

The assistants had to be fluent in multiple languages, those which covered all crafts and all the tools of such crafts. They were often men of a certain age and looked particularly well-informed and experienced. Their uniform of long brown laboratory-style coats, with pens and a small steel rule in the top pocket, underlined their status as consultants to the trade world, oracles to be consulted and befriended.

The latter aspect was a particular feature of men's shops of this kind. I think men like to belong to tribes and what better one than an exclusive tribe of tradesmen? Most introductory greetings, I noticed, would contain some reference to Fred or Bill and if they'd been in the shop recently. This shop is where the brothers of the secret fraternity met.

I was always pleased to enter this shop with my father, who had been a cabinet maker; he could announce with confidence which tools he'd like to look at. It was not infrequent that I would be a little confused by this, because during our walk to town I would naturally ask him what he wanted to buy and his reply would be in everyday English, such as 'a plane'. This seemed simple enough, but once in the shop, the secret words of greeting having been passed across the counter, he would then ask for something such as 'a bullnose rabbet with inverted oval mortise'. We would depart with the tool wrapped in brown paper, my pride in my father's secret linguistic abilities increased.

In department stores, customers were attended by assistants who addressed them with perhaps excessive respect and a certain fawning manner. They gave the impression that they were looking for rich customers and were deciding which one was going to spend money by the clothes they wore. A genuine fur coat would attract attention from their practiced eyes, most fur coats being expensive. Even being seen browsing in James Howells gave women, a certain cachet with their neighbours. "I saw her in Howells the other day, I didn't know she could afford it."

Ironmonger's shop

Both men and women would therefore go to town, or to the cinema, not only wearing their best clothes, but also their best hats.

Trilbies were popular for the men, flat caps being marginally frowned upon for these excursions. Caps should be kept for work; a form of faux-middle class behaviour was felt to be the correct aspiration for everyone, along with universal politeness. The holding open of doors, standing up on a bus or tram for a woman, for example, were standard courtesies to be practiced on such occasions.

One may question why this politeness and respect was shown to women. We should not forget that at this time, although most men worked very hard for very long hours, it was recognised that women had a difficult time too and were on the whole to be protected and looked out for. This may seem patronising, but it was not. Manners and politeness counted for a lot in families. An ill-mannered boy would bring embarrassment on the family and he would be disciplined for it. He must learn to look out for those who could benefit from simple kindnesses.

To many men, to venture out without their hat was something they hardly ever did, even in the height of summer. It was generally felt that to cover the head was something advisable, not only for fashion, but for health. The sun was seen as harmful and a bare head was to be protected. For some reason, a bare head was frowned upon, as though a male head, especially a partially bald one, was something that was best hidden. Removing one's hat when meeting someone or entering a building enabled the wearer to demonstrate their respect for the place or for the person they were meeting.

My grandfather, along with many other allotment workers, would be seen working at the soil, sleeves rolled up, waistcoat on and wearing a hat.

The use of a hat has not entirely died out, of course. Today, many a farmer doesn't feel whole unless he has a flat hat on his head, the occasional removal of which then reveals a line above which the head is quite white, over a sun-browned forehead.

We boys didn't wear waistcoats of course, but our clothing was in some ways different to today's. We wore short trousers with long socks until we were about twelve. The move to wearing long trousers was something of a rite of passage and most secondary schools had very clear rules as to the earliest this should be done. In our school, it was when we entered Form 3.

Blazers were standard wear for boys. Not only did our schools require us to wear one, of various colours (and sometimes patterns), but they were generally felt to be a pretty good garment for all-round wear. When I was about six years old, I remember having a bright red one for Sunday School. Was I proud! No problem finding me in a crowd. And a cap was seen as just as important for us boys to wear as they were for men.

The war changed many things, not least of all the role of women. Those who had successfully contributed to the war effort by working in factories had opened up the question of why their role was still seen, by men, as being in the home. When men who had survived the war returned and demanded their jobs back, ousting the women who had been doing them, there was naturally resentment from women and understandably so.

Once the 60s burst upon us, the young challenged the status quo with their clothes. Teddy boys, for example, with their long, Edwardian jackets, their suede-covered shoes with thick crepe soles, affronted many older people, whose poor opinion of them was confirmed when some of them formed violent gangs.

When Carnaby Street fashions appeared, with their unusual colours, their geometric shapes and the wearing of miniskirts, older folk thought the world had come to an end. Women were not only debating their role but also breaking social taboos and signalling their disaffection with tradition via their clothing. Suddenly, the world was inhabited and being led by young people, not the old and experienced, whose thrones were being shaken.

But back to hats... where did they all come from? Well, there were a number of milliners' shops in Cardiff, serving both men and women. The largest women's one was Marments. It was a wonderful, elegant shop: very large and spacious, with Greco-Roman pillars supporting the front of the stone building, which is still there, but occupied now by ubiquitous franchises.

It had a huge curving staircase on the right hand side of the entrance that took shoppers to the first floor where the most strange and ultra-fashionable hats were to be found.

Surveying the first floor as a child, there seemed to be hats floating on air. What I mean is, the hats were not just left on shelves;

Site of Marments' shop

they were placed on chrome stands of various heights and angles, so that a small boy would see them high up and supported all over the shop, as though they were floating in mid-air. The whole floor resembled the ascent of a group of hot air balloons. Buying one required at least one assistant and perhaps the best part would be its wrapping and boxing. I sometimes wondered whether the box was the best part of having a hat.

For men, there was Jothams, Calders, Roberts and Davies, all having dedicated hat departments. The hats had lovely satin linings and the hat had to be 'steamed' into shape. A steam generator emitted steam through a chrome nozzle which was directed at the felt hat and enabled it to be bent into the shape required – sometimes pulling down the front a little (giving a more rakish effect) or perhaps bending the rear up a little so as to avoid rain dripping down your neck. It was fascinating to watch, the transaction being completed with a thorough brushing of the felt and of course the crumpling of large volumes of tissue paper which filled the hat whilst in its box.

When I was eighteen, my father thought it was time that I had a hat. So he took me to Roberts, on the corner of Queen Street and Kingsway, not only to get a hat but also a new overcoat. I liked the overcoat, but didn't really see myself in a hat, especially the Robin-Hood shaped one that my father chose for me. It came to a peak in front, turned up at the back and had a feather in it. Honestly!

But I couldn't bring myself to deny him the obvious pleasure he had in seeing me as a well-dressed 'man about town'. To be honest, I was too embarrassed to wear it and once out of the house I used to carry the hat as nonchalantly as possible in my hand, as though it was something I had just found lying on the pavement.

But the hat was only one item of adornment to which women devoted careful attention: hats often had veils which could be pulled down especially when in church, almost as though they were removing visual temptation from male eyes.

A neighbour of ours, a Mrs S, who was already an elderly lady when I was young and of an earlier generation than my parents, was a particularly dedicated practitioner of dressing with decorum. She not only pulled down her veil on Sundays, but in the summer her otherwise bare arms (perhaps another temptation to male eyes) would be covered by very long lace gloves, which reached right up to her armpits. When we met her in the street, I would study these strange gloves at very close quarters as she talked with my mother.

They were made of complex lace patterns, closely stitched around the hands, and with a more open pattern higher up, with sewn-on miniature flowers here and there. By far the most striking feature of them was the huge numbers of holes in the lace weave and weft, so that I wondered what the point was; the gloves contained precious little material at all, and were mainly holes!

But the gloves did cover her arms without causing her, the wearer, discomfort in warm weather and I suppose this was the point. These, together with her veil, attached to her wide-brimmed hat, with her Bible clasped in her gloved hands and with a lightweight handbag covered in matching lace-like material made it clear that she took great care to dress well on Sundays.

We can see from these observations of dress that in the 40s and 50s there remained a clear echo of the Edwardian past, which would be swept away for young people by the new and audacious fashions of the 1960s.

***

Mrs S was very religious and she started a club for young children which she held in her front room every Tuesday evening. It was The Good News Club. My brother and I, together with Christine and Paul from next door, used to go to it, where we'd be told stories from the Bible illustrated not with a Powerpoint presentation but with the aid of a green felt board to which felt figures were stuck as the stories unfolded. A hymn to finish, sometimes with clapping and joyous Hallelujahs enlivened our Tuesday evenings.

If most of such evenings were of a quiet and respectful tone as we listened sitting on the floor to Bible stories, these last happy-clappy songs, shouting to the world how happy we were, gave us an opportunity to release some of our energy, the lead for which was given by Mrs S on her poor piano.

I write 'poor' because the instrument was beyond tuning, according to my father, because of having a wooden frame. It was unable to hold a tune even if someone attempted it. Basically, Mrs S produced such a loud noise on this instrument, hermetically sealed as we were in her small front room, that none of us could just sit there in silence; although I think some of the neighbours wished we would, for not everyone wanted to hear *Sing a Song for Jesus* at full volume.

Her piano-playing technique was worthy of note. I can only describe it as being of the 'hit-it-like-hell' school, consisting of a terrifying vertical attack on the poor instrument's keyboard. The relatively lightweight instrument (because of its wooden frame) would react not only with the most agonising sounds, but also by performing frightening physical movements as it rocked back and fore, threatening to fall forward onto the pianist and us assembled on the floor. Boy, could she exert a downward thrust on that poor instrument, the top of which had to be cleared of loose items before she struck up!

Such a technique required muscular effort of a significant kind; the manic movements of her flailing arms demonstrating the total commitment she gave these happy songs. If we weren't happy, she was! Spare flesh, mainly hanging from her upper arms, would exhibit rhythmic ripples as the underlying muscles smashed her hands into the keyboard. These ripples, resembling the rippling of material when air first enters an empty hot air balloon, were totally mesmerizing to me, as she hit hell out of the old tuneless piano; but she did so with such gusto that the clanking and 'donging' of the poor dumb instrument was irrelevant, her muscular performance being a distraction in itself.

It was as if she thought that sheer physical force would make the instrument play the right tune, even if its rusted strings refused to do so. Add to the fascinating performance of her arms, a loud contralto voice which screamed above the noise, and you may be able to understand that the final happy-clappy song was something we eagerly looked forward to. She really was giving it her all and we'd better follow suit.

Mrs S also demonstrated her uniquely muscular style of playing during the Coronation street party. A rostrum had been constructed half-way down our street, lights had been strung across the road and flags poked out of windows in June 1953. It was on this rostrum, bedecked with bunting, that her poor piano had been installed. Above it, the front of the instrument having been removed, was suspended a huge chrome microphone, of the sort seen in old movies. Loud speakers transmitted her playing to the rest of the street and far beyond.

After renditions of several patriotic tunes such as *Jerusalem* (she also ran the W.I.) and *There'll be Blue Birds Over the White Cliffs of Dover* she gave up in sheer exhaustion and my father was asked to play something to which people could sing and dance, which he did, our family losing him to this task for many hours afterwards.

My extended family is shown in the photograph, taken at the Coronation street party, my brother being in my mother's arms, she seated to the right of my father, then grandmother and grandfather.

The reason I'm inserting this anecdote here, is that Mrs S's dress sense reached its zenith on this celebratory day. Not only was one of her large, flower-covered hats worn at the most jaunty angle, but her long lace gloves were used too, with handkerchiefs stuffed into bracelets at several points. Boy, was she ready to party! After all, as the unelected and self-appointed Mistress of Ceremonies, she had to look well dressed.

To round off this memory, I note that the street party was a really wonderful event, singing and dancing lasting long into the night (all children being allowed to stay up late if they were able), fuelled by my father's playing accompanied by an uncle of ours and others.

Actually, Dad switched fairly early to his accordion, because the rostrum, being in the middle of the street and the party being at our end, he was marooned seemingly miles away from everyone else on a deserted island, with only Mrs S's eccentric piano for company. I remember him walking back to the party's Ground Zero from his remote, deserted rostrum mumbling something such as:

"I don't know what's going on; I can't hear myself play because the speakers are down here and I'm up there and that piano is getting the better of me."

My brother and I entered the fancy dress competition at the party. I was dressed as PC 49 (a well-known police constable hero) and Brian was Davy Crocket, King of the Wild Frontier. I can't remember who won the competition, but I know that we didn't; a disappointment that scarred us for life.

Coronation street party in Penhevad Street

CHAPTER FIFTEEN
Not Today, Thank You

Many commodities were delivered to our front doors: groceries, milk, pop, etc.; but, not all such service providers called at our request. Many cold callers came, trying to sell products which they often gave us to believe had almost magical properties. Listening to the rapid, non-stop, theatrical 'gab' of these salesmen (they were usually men, except for gypsies) was an experience I revelled in. I would stand there literally with my mouth open in amazement – something that would annoy my mother who would sometimes close it. More annoying to her was that I was showing an intense interest in the salesman – an opinion not usually shared by her, who just wanted to close the door.

Betterware salesman

Thus it was that the visits of door-to-door salesmen would offer us products which, they claimed, would transform our lives – but only if we bought them for cash, there and then, on the doorstep, before these revolutionary products ever got to the shops, there to be bought by everyone else (and by implication, by those not able to enjoy the unique privilege he was bestowing on us, of being the very first to see them). We were offered brushes that would never wear out; shoes that would never let in water; chimney products that ensured our chimneys never needed sweeping; amazing American gadgets that would enable us to slice five cucumbers a minute (if ever we wanted to); gadgets to sharpen knives, polish cutlery, clean windows, add life to a dead battery, plug holes in leaking car radiators and so on.

The company with salesmen 'par excellence' was Betterware and they were known as the Betterware Men. The original name of the company was Betterwear, but this was changed to Betterware in the 1960s and is still trading today.

These cheerful chaps would drag the most enormous, often brightly coloured, suitcases all over Grangetown, at the same time clutching numerous mops, Ostrich-feathered dusters and yard brushes; so that when one of them aimed his talents at a particular house, the unsuspecting resident could tell who was about to knock on the front door by the clatter of falling brushes, mops and gadgets together with the inevitable thump of a heavy suitcase.

Parents often sent their children to answer the door so as not to be trapped into buying something by the clever sales patter of these people. But that didn't work; they were ready for any eventuality, having trained for many years, I'm sure, in places like Pontypridd Market, an institution in itself which we often visited. Seeing a child's face peeping round the door would be met with a simple question: "Is your mother in, sonny? What's your mother's name?"

No boy could answer 'I don't know' and the trap was sprung. Or, if I had been told to tell a lie, such as "Mam's busy" they might respond with, "Oh I know, mothers are always busy, aren't they? But I'm sure your mam wouldn't mind me having a glass of water – do you think you could get one for me?" What mother would then dispatch their son with such a thing to a stranger on the door without making an appearance herself?

To avoid this obvious doorstep bit of theatrical licence, my mother used to buy something small, anything, just to get rid of a Betterware man – it was often something shamefully cheap such as a duster; anything just to get back to normal life, because once these people had opened their blue case, you were stuck to them like Brer Rabbit to the Tar Baby.

The suitcase, however, was rarely opened immediately. A rapport had to be built up first, over subjects such as the weather or even how nice our house looked: "I can see you take a pride in your home and this is why I've chosen to call on you today."

Eventually, after some softening up, the magic suitcase would be opened, with great ceremony, its enormity suddenly becoming apparent to small yet bulging eyes like mine. Sometimes folding out into three sections, it was no ordinary suitcase. Within it, seemingly

Advertisement for Lifebuoy Soap

hundreds of items were cleverly fixed into their unique places. It was like opening a magic box that transformed itself into a shop, right in front of my eyes. It must have been very heavy. No wonder the poor Betterware Men were tired and somewhat depressed when not on a doorstep, sometimes to be found leaning disconsolately up against a wall having a cigarette.

Pegs, yellow dusters, Flit fly spray, mop heads, soap, polishes of all kinds for all occasions, knives, knife sharpeners, tea cosies, ant powder, DDT cockroach powder, dubbin, black lead for the fire grate, graphite paste, blue bags for bleaching the washing, string... All this was available from this bottomless case as if produced by a wizard and that's what he was trying to be. Rather than deter the man, I was frequently the cause of him staying much longer than he might have if I hadn't been there. And as if to make me a future buyer, he would sometimes produce a toffee or a sweet lollipop to bribe my future investment in him.

I admit that any salesmen who had 'the gift of the gab' were always a magnet for me, whether they were on the margins of funfairs, selling from the back of large enclosed lorries, or in fixed markets such as that in central Cardiff (Mill Lane) or the best and largest of them all at Pontypridd. To see these men throwing plates and cups into the air, juggling them in large numbers, clattering them together to demonstrate their robustness, then stacking them up:

"Not six places, not eight, but twelve, I give you a twelve-place dinner service, ladies and gentlemen, not for £15, don't even offer me £10; yes, this twelfth-place dinner service, modelled on the best England can make...not £15, not £10 – who'll give me a fiver for the lot?" went the theatrical patter. "There you are, one lucky lady over

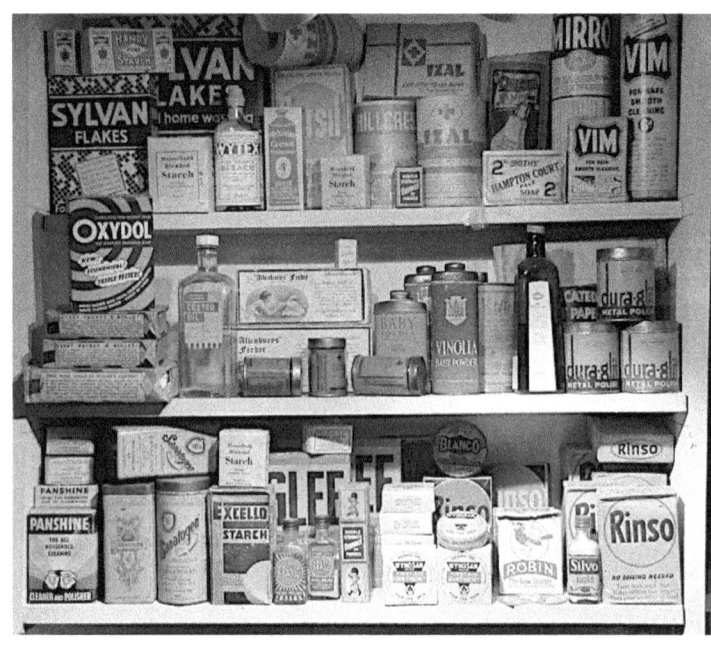

Miscellaneous products of the era

Dubbin

Stove blacking

Flit fly-spray pump

there; love you've been so good to take the first set, just give me a quid and it's yours!"

What?! A pound for all that crockery, we'd ask ourselves, gasping at the bargain. The truth usually was that she was the tradesman's wife or girlfriend. Then a rush would take place as the crowd thought they'd spotted a bargain (they thought!) and hands would shoot up with money in them. Word would go around that a special bargain could be had at the back of this lorry. Sadly, but predictably, little or nothing would be gained by buying crockery in this way, because it needed very careful examination, something the salesmen would rarely allow.

These men were worth staring at. Throwing rolled-up rugs and carpets out over the heads of the crowd; slapping the unopened bags of sheets as the price was slashed; pretending to quarrel with a colleague who was often standing in the back of the lorry or stall, pretending to be the sensible one, begging the salesman not to cut the price any more or they'd be broke...throwing in pillows if you bought a sheet...so the patter went on and on and on...

"Don't give me a quid, not even ten bob, don't even think of five bob; I'll tell you what, I'll give this carpet to the first person up 'ere with a bob in his 'and. I can't do better than that – besides, my partner is already telling me we're losing money on these things, but they've got to go! I don't care if we lose money today, as long as you're 'appy, I'm 'appy!"

It was the best street theatre and it was free. They were very talented showmen and the excitement they instilled in me made the day out well worthwhile. The trouble was, I could rarely tear myself away from them and often lost my parents who had departed ages ago.

There were other, more essential, visitors too; one was a Mr Adams, the insurance man. He came weekly, usually on a Tuesday afternoon, to collect the few shillings that my parents and grandparent were investing in life and house assurances. He always wore a trilby hat, even in summer, the warm season being advertised by him relinquishing his brown mackintosh.

He was an odd man: he seemed to specialise in making strange noises for the amusement of children and since I was always (stupidly) grinning he seemed to find me a willing target for his latest voice or strange sound.

His favourite voice was to speak like a tiny girl he called Mary Jane who he reckoned lived in his pocket. I suppose this contrast of size was a bit amusing, since Mr Adams was about 6 feet tall; but I think after a few years of being entertained to these strange voices and Mary Jane's opinions it was wearing a bit thin.

He tried to be a ventriloquist, but was rather bad at it. Talking to a coat pocket was, frankly, peculiar. I've no idea how this talent related to insurance. My mother would sigh a sigh of relief once he'd gone, but it was her fault he stayed so long; she always offered him a cup of tea, to be thanked by Mary Jane who each week was apparently dying of thirst. Listening to him imitating this imaginary miniature girl slurping tea whilst she was still in his pocket was something I should really have refused to be involved in, but I couldn't help being sympathetic to him, who although he was clearly mad, was at least trying.

He took only seconds to mark the insurance books with the small amounts we paid and then seemed to spend ages sipping the tea. He used the hot tea as an excuse to continue making odd noises and speaking strangely, in Mary Jane's voice, even when thanking my mother for the tea. Even saying goodbye as he walked to the front door would be executed in the same way, speaking as though he was Mary Jane. How odd! But I used to laugh at him every time, although it was wearing rather thin by the time I was eighteen.

Another regular, strange and funny visitor, was Arthur. He had been a professional boxer (lightweight) but had to retire when the sport was evidently affecting his brain. He spoke rapidly and unclearly but always with a joke and a strong laugh attached to it. He never kept still and was often just bouncing around a little, as though shadow boxing. He used to pop in for a cup of tea, with many tales to tell, especially when he got a job at the Gas Board (as it used to be). He was employed to cut off the gas supply to houses where the residents had got into arrears with their bills. I suppose the company thought that an ex-boxer would be a good sort of chap to use for this unsavoury service.

One can imagine the sort of situation into which he got: Neanderthal house-owners trying to stop him; wives screaming abuse; old age pensioners and children crying. Lovely job! We often asked him how he could do it and he always responded that it's their fault for not paying, which is fair comment I suppose.

Sometimes he would relate that he had to get at least two people to go along with him to cut off the gas supply to a house where the inhabitants were particularly ferocious and sometimes the police were needed. He described the crafty tactics he used to distract the attention of the householder, such as sending his assistants around the back of the house to try and gain entry whilst he and a policeman broke in through the front door and quickly cut off the gas, attaching a seal to the meter.

Perhaps those cups of tea he used to call for at our house may have been to help him after the trauma of such an entry, although he never showed any nervousness about what he did, quite the contrary. He seemed to enjoy his work, although I noticed that he used to bounce around and his head twitch more after an exciting day.

Arthur was also interesting because of his love life. He'd married once and according to him the divorce cost him a fortune in a settlement; a fact that affected how he felt about ever getting married again. But this didn't stop him from having numerous girlfriends and it was tales of his latest adventures which I know intrigued my mother, especially.

When going courting, he could strike quite a handsome pose: shining Brylcreemed hair and smart suits were his fashion, with the most shiny shoes you can imagine; he had been a corporal in the army after the war. But his secret weapon he reckoned was his car(s). He seemed to be constantly changing his car and usually had the largest and most chrome-covered vehicles imaginable. Since the gas company gave him a van in which to ply his depressing trade, his car was free for romancing purposes. Always brilliantly polished, spotlessly clean and with a small cushion on the passenger seat ('they like that little bit of comfort') he seemed a little like the iconic character Alfie in the film of the same name, featuring Michael Caine. A bit of a 'spiv' was our Arthur! Smart ties, the finest clothes and shoes, a smart car and 'treated 'em nice', he did.

I'm not really sure how we got to know him; perhaps he was linked to my grandfather via the gas company that they both worked for. My grandfather also liked boxing so perhaps that was a second link. But whilst it was reasonable for him to come and relate some of his work-a-day stories to us, at times it seemed a little embarrassing to go over his latest romantic conquests. He was a brilliant dancer, small though he was, at barely 5 feet tall. For me, it wasn't his tales of romance that were interesting, it was the way he told them, his head twitching and his body shadow boxing.

We sometimes had gypsies call on us. They were usually women: wild, dark-skinned women, whom one never wanted to cross. They often wore elaborate head scarves wound in a peculiar way around their heads and reminded me of Spanish dancers; and of course they wore large ear-rings. They carried their wares in a large wicker basket, the handle of which was supported through one arm whilst the other proffered some flowers, usually 'lucky' heather. They also sold wooden clothes pegs which were usually the items we purchased most.

The women were, quite frankly, not comfortable people to welcome on the doorstep and I was certainly frightened by them. My grandmother said that if we bought nothing from them they would cast a curse on us, so we usually did. She was quite superstitious.

Their reputation for crime also influenced my impression of them, an impression for which my grandfather was responsible. He told us tales of wanton damage and the theft of significant amounts of produce from his allotment; so this too made me feel that these visitors to our doorstep were not welcome ones, especially when one noticed that as the women knocked on doors in the street, their dangerous-looking menfolk kept watch in various doorways.

I had reason to be somewhat scared of gypsies when attacked by a small band of their children as I was out playing in the woods. My brother and a friend of ours A and myself had cycled there to improve our den; a hide-out in a tree, the branches of which overhung an escarpment, making it impregnable from that side. But the gypsy children had other ideas and as we left the den, they followed us and ambushed us.

I freely admit to being very frightened by these dirty and obviously pugnacious children; but I was made of stern stuff and was determined not to give in to intimidation. So I gave them my best penknife!

CHAPTER SIXTEEN
Money Singing on Wires

When I think of some of the gadgets and equipment that were used when I was young they now make me smile. One such example, which fascinated me so much that my mother had to drag me away from watching it, was the way cash was managed in some shops.

There were two methods of handling cash (hardly anyone used cheques and of course cards had not been invented): either the assistant placed the money in a mechanical till (more or less like now, but simpler), or the customer went with a receipt to pay at a central desk, often high up and surrounded by glass or a metal grill, the cashier being imprisoned, zoo-like, in a cage.

The designers of such shops seemed to think that shop assistants were either not trusted or not intelligent enough to be able to handle cash; so others, sealed off in a cage, had to do it. This method was not very user-friendly, the shopper having to walk to this central 'counting house' and back again to collect their goods once they had paid for them. If you were under 5 feet tall, like my mother, trying to pay at the central cash desk could even be a little embarrassing, as such desks were often about 5 feet tall. It seemed as though she was begging for leniency before a judge, or had approached some sacred altar, a penitent wishing to make a gift to the god within.

Two stores, at least, felt that sending customers to this rather unfriendly cash island to pay for their purchases could be improved upon. So they designed systems that would enable sales assistants to send a customer's money to this central elves' vault and by return have a receipt without the customer having to move. One method was pneumatic, and this is still used in Tesco's today. James Howells first installed a vacuum system, whereby the cash and the receipt were both placed in a cylinder which was sucked up into a pipe and sent to the elves somewhere in the upper floors of the shop.

But the most fascinating system for me was the one used at Peacocks in Canton. This clothes shop was a lovely one to visit, not only because of the system I'll describe, but also because it had the noisiest, creakiest wooden floors I've ever experienced. It seemed as though most of the floorboards had gradually lifted on their nails so that anyone walking over them made loud creaking and cracking noises. Naturally, a boy like me spent most of his time when there, making this noise appear from different parts of the shop and in particular discovering the parts of the floor where the noise was loudest. My mother reckoned she never needed to look for me because she just walked to where these loud creaking noises were coming from and there I was.

The Peacocks system was an ingenious one whereby each counter was linked to the central elves' bank by an overhead wire, at the ends of which was a spring. Any change and eventually the receipt were placed in a brass pot with a screw top and hooked onto the wire in a small basket. The assistant, or on its return an elf, would pull a handle attached by a chord to a spring-loaded mechanism at either end of the wire, a catch would release, and hit the brass pot, sending it whizzing along its wire to the other end. A shopper could trace the trajectory of his or her money as it zoomed to and from the elves' enclave. If you were a young lad, you could even try and out-run it, dodging in and out of aisles as the brass pot travelled overhead making a whizzing noise.

You could also see just how long you had to wait, because the pots, when arriving at the elves' cave would hang there, their tops having been unscrewed and parked waiting for the elves to sort out the change and send them back. Then, 'whizzzzz', back came the pot, returning with the change and a stamped receipt.

Of course all these wires made the store look a little odd, rather like a miniature ski resort, but a suitable coating of brass on most of the components made them shine and shimmer as the system operated. It was all very simple to maintain and no money could ever get lost, because each pot could be seen clearly at all points on its trajectory. Once, one of our pots got stuck because it lost too much speed when it bumped into a display that someone was putting up; but it was soon rescued and off it went again, whizzing on its way, like a homing pigeon returning to its loft. It was such a simple system that needed no electricity and was amusing at the same time - at least for nosey children it was.

Dylan Thomas, in *Under Milk Wood*, mentions this method of transporting cash when describing an emporium "where money sang on wires". I wonder if he ever visited Peacocks?

Previous to the invention of the transistor, wireless sets used either thermionic valve-powered circuits, or the smallest sets were crystal ones, requiring headphones. Ignoring crystals, which were dying out except for amateur radio builders like myself, valve radios consumed huge amounts of electricity because the valves became hot. In order to run a portable radio of this kind required batteries that were powerful. Lead-acid batteries, of the same design but smaller than those used in cars (6 volts not 12), were needed. They were very heavy, their cases being of thick glass, and dangerous, containing as they did sulphuric acid. To short-circuit one was to cause an explosion.

In spite of these dangers and inconveniences, the portable radio was catching on and it was felt the height of sophistication to be able to listen to a wireless when, say, on a beach or in a park. But the batteries didn't last long and had to be frequently reinvigorated. It was we children who were often tasked with taking these things to be re-charged at an ironmongers where they were left on charge overnight before being collected the next day. Sometimes the ironmonger would also top up the acid if needed. He checked whether it was charged, not by measuring its voltage but by measuring the specific gravity of the acid. All this required a special area in the shop where batteries and acid could be safely handled.

The batteries were made of heavy glass (the electrodes being clearly visible) and transported by means of a steel frame that passed around the neck of the square glass bottle and then attached to a wooden carrying-handle. I mention all this detail to show that it was impossible to carry a so-called portable radio as we do today (perhaps tucked into a pocket, or a bag): both it and its lead-acid battery were far too heavy. Going for a picnic with such a radio required a little bit of planning and preparation and even when used, its period of use was limited, before the battery ran out.

The comparison with today's electronic gadgets that we are able to carry around in our pockets is striking. They are now so small we hardly feel their weight and they work for days before needing re-charging. More to the point, they offer us instant communication. This was something unthought of sixty years ago. Few homes on our island had telephones and even using a public phone box would not allow international calls unless they had been previously booked.

If anything was urgent or important and needed long distance communication (by which I mean from Cardiff to London and beyond) then telegrams were the only means. These meant a visit to the central post office where we would fill out a telegram message form, using as few words as possible. Local post offices did not always handle telegrams because a transmitter/receiver and an operator were required. The words were counted and we paid according to the number we'd written.

It would then go to the telegraph room where it would be transmitted by Morse code to the destination, where our words would be printed out on a strip of paper tape that would be cut into suitable lengths for pasting onto a telegram form. The telegram would be hand delivered at its intended destination by a telegram boy.

We were not far from the central post office, so telegrams were indeed delivered by boys on bikes. For deliveries further afield the post office used men on motorbikes. Telegrams could be things to be feared. They were sent only on special occasions, both happy and sad, but too many during and after the war were ones announcing a wounding or a death. To see a telegram boy appear in the street was a sight of some concern.

GPO Telegram motorbike

Another gadget worthy of comparison with what we enjoy today was the gramophone. Although my grandparents used to have a gramophone with a horn, my parents had an electrical one. I'd better describe both of these.

During my grandparents' lifetimes, records were still a novelty. My grandmother was quite a collector, usually buying records from Spillers' Music Shop in town (claimed to be the world's oldest record shop). Whilst it was true that the original wax cylinders had long been superseded by Bakelite records, the principle whereby the imprinted sound was amplified remained the same.

A steel needle ran in the grooves of sound which had been imprinted into the record, and the needle's vibrations were passed to a hardened but very thin, steel diaphragm, which was mounted at the narrow end of a large horn. The horn was made of paper, hardened with 'dope' or very thin varnish. (Some were elaborately decorated with flowers, abstract patterns or just made to look metallic.) The horn, diaphragm and needle were all lifted onto the record as it turned, so the assembly had to be light.

The mechanism for turning the record beneath the needle was originally mechanical; the user turned a handle which was connected to a spring which, when released, drove a clockwork mechanism at the chosen speed. So playing records was something which required preparation and a little exercise too.

Initially, there seems to have been little or no standardization as to the diameter, thickness or the speed of records. I remember that my grandmother's collection contained a miscellany of discs: some were very thin, others thick, some were only 3 or 4 inches in diameter, others more like 10 inches. So getting this right was not obvious and the record players had to accommodate all the permutations of size and speed.

Later, during my father's youth, electrical motors drove the turntable but not everyone had electricity. We were lucky to have electricity by the late 1940s and we also had two wireless sets, one of which (a dark brown Bakelite one) had connections at the back into which the electrical output from a magnetic sound head could be plugged. These magnetic sound heads, which replaced the diaphragm of my grandmother's generation of record players, were in fact just crude modifications of telephone earpieces and/or headphones; but they did the job.

Many of my younger days (until, say, twelve) were spent lying on the floor of the front room, surrounded by tall stacks of records and playing one after the other on either of the gramophones we had: either my grandmother's great horn type (which was amusing) or my father's. Tommy Dorsey, Glen Miller, Billy Cotton, Count Basey, Grapelli, Reinhard, and so on, were all available to me. What jazz riches! But my record-playing sessions caused a problem for others, notably my grandfather. I needed to steal the wireless from the living room to play the records and come the one o'clock news, my grandfather's sacred ritual, I was not popular if the wireless was not available.

* * *

As an aside, I had a rich aunt, who I visited several times. I could tell she was rich because she cut sandwiches into triangular quarters and removed the crusts. She also had a fountain in her very large garden, which was near Roath Park lake. The house and the garden were very different to our terraced house with its back yard. The idea of having grass near the house wasn't really practiced much in Grangetown, whereas residents of the lakeside area were obviously keen on the idea.

Drinking tea from a delicate china cup, complete with a saucer is quite an impressive experience when very young. I was clearly in the presence of royalty and I made sure I washed my hands before eating and tried not to eat too much.

My aunt had no fewer than *three* pianolas in her spacious front room. These were actual pianos which played music from a piano roll, inserted into them. The rolls contained holes that when detected would operate each piano key. She had a large library of them, many by great composers and pianists, such as Rachmaninoff. The mechanism was operated by pumping pedals which opened out from beneath the instrument. When retracted, the piano could be played as a normal one.

These instruments were very expensive and were of a high quality so that the sound I could generate from them was very impressive, especially when compared with the basic piano we had.

Pianola piano

* * *

The need for an amplifier for the record player was urgent if I was to continue to listen my way through the enormous collection of records we had. So I experimented in making a few, usually by buying the parts from an Aladdin's cave of electrical parts, which were on sale in the Wyndham Arcade. I could buy anything I wanted for pennies from this amazing shop, which bought its stock from the War Ministry (as was). It was surplus to the war effort and I could get all I needed once I'd understood the electrical circuits, which I researched in the reference section of the central library.

The shop was also a good source of parts for making my own radios, Morse code sets, short-wave radios, amplifiers, my very first tiny TV set (it had a cathode ray tube only 3 inches in diameter) and even an electro-mechanical computer (Babbage watch out), which worked after a fashion – at least it did crude arithmetic for me albeit taking an age of clanking and clicking.

This shop made me realise just how much 'kit' the Americans provided for the war. Much of what I used in my circuits were actually American parts, which meant looking up the equivalent in UK specifications, which wasn't always easy. Measured by the amount of equipment on sale in that shop, I got the impression the UK fought the war with mainly American equipment.

One day, after months of reading, calculating and head-scratching, and clouds of smelly solder that rose from a huge soldering-iron that was better designed for making saucepans than attaching fine wires, I was ready to switch on my first amplifier. I remember waiting until everyone was out of the house and placed the very heavy and very large assembly on the table in the middle room. Connecting (cotton-covered) cable to it and a suitable round-pin plug, I retreated behind the middle room door and gingerly plugged it in. I flicked the switch using a broom handle – that's how confident I was! And it hummed and glowed into life! Wow! A living 'thing', had been created. I was so proud and excited.

Now to plug in the gramophone. The outcome of this next phase (the ultimate goal) was not so good. My creation was amplifying the sound alright but it also amplified a horrendous mains hum of fifty cycles per second.

I not only gained a lot of experience in the design and construction of electrical gadgets, but I also gained my independence from my grandfather's wireless. I was now free to listen to records whenever I wished, mains hum and all.

The construction of this amplifier also got me interested in radio. I built a wireless set based on the electromagnetic resonance of a crystal (can't remember which type) under mechanical pressure.

The power output was puny and could only be picked up by sensitive earphones, but it was a lovely little thing. Because most sets of that era were not able to amplify high frequency signals very cleanly, it was important to provide them with as strong an input signal as possible. Most back yards therefore boasted high and sometimes elaborate wireless aerials, which were just lengths of wire running from the house to, say, the top of the washing line and insulated from both by china insulators. These presented lightning with a wonderfully attractive target and there were often cases in the news of wireless sets, just like mine, having been blown up by a lightning strike. Naturally, when persuading my parents and grandparents to let me climb up the washing line's pole to fasten my aerial to its top, none of these risks were mentioned.

Then came my first valve wireless – only one valve, but it was a beauty. Dad made a wooden frame on which to mount all the bits (a condenser-tuner, a large resonant capacitor and power and grid bias circuits) and it worked first time. Again, it was of low power, but ran on a very large dry battery, which meant that I could take it to bed and listen to it there. It was lovely to listen to Alistair Cooke's original *Letter from America* transmissions and *Our Hundred Best Tunes*, both of which were broadcast on a Sunday evening; me not wanting to go to sleep in spite of there being school in the morning. Perhaps it was from these broadcasts, received over my very own wireless circuits, that I still retain a deep love of wireless and much prefer it to television.

My favourite wireless programmes were part of Children's Hour, from 5 to 6pm. It was introduced by 'Uncle Mac', who had a particularly pleasant and comforting voice, one which I can clearly recall now. His goodbye was particularly memorable as he said each time: "Goodbye, children – goodbye children, everywhere." I felt as though I was part of a (global, if only empire-wide) network of children, containing as it did, episodes of *Toytown* where Larry the Lamb (who spoke in a tremulous voice) interacted with Mr Mayor, Mr Grouser and Captain Brass.

You could buy books based on the programme, such as *Uncle Mac's Children's Hour*, or *Jennings Goes to School* (schoolboy pranks) or episodes of *Jeff Arnold and Riders of the Range* (cowboys of course). These serialisations were mostly available as books and the latter one I had, I remember.

The broadcasts had different themes according to the days of the week and reflected the pace and social context of the day. Sundays, for example, had a more contemplative atmosphere to them and was written for the whole family to listen to, not only children. It frequently featured biographical plays and historical dramas; competitions, or programmes designed to stimulate a career choice. The *I Want to Be...* programme was a favourite of mine, featuring each week a different job and interviewing those who had them – policemen, firemen, doctors, scientists, etc. A far cry from today's 'I want to be a celebrity'.

Monday's editions were more adventurous and I think in two parts: the first half hour was devoted to the really young and the second half to older children. This would contain reviews of films, theatre productions, talks on music and sport and politics. It was quality listening. Wednesdays, I remember, was a special day in that it featured a serial and perhaps the results of various competitions. Thursdays was devoted largely, but not entirely, to reviewing books – *For Your Bookshelf*. Compared to today's hysterical 'shows' where little or no intellectual effort is required, *Children's Hour* was sophisticated, mirroring adult programmes. Children were not talked down to, but were treated as young, intelligent adults.

We listened to *Children's Hour*, especially the Sunday edition, with my grandparents who lived in the middle room of the house. Sunday would have been a quiet, slow day of Sunday School and church-going, habitually rounded off with a light tea during *Children's Hour*. We might even have tinned peaches and condensed milk with thin slices of bread as a treat.

My grandfather had a particular penchant for cheese-on-toast on these occasions, or perhaps pikelets, which he toasted over the fire with a toasting fork. What a lovely smell they gave off. And how scrumptious they became as the butter melted into them!

That smell, with the familiar and reassuring calm of Sundays was a wonderful gift to us children. *Children's Hour* ended in 1964, to a huge uproar of protest, perhaps marking the end of innocence for both our child's world as well as the adult one. That year also saw the blockade of Cuba, the Panama Canal crisis, the shooting down of a US spy plane, the Vietnam War continuing and the Cold War reaching a dangerous climax.

Saturday evenings were also a wireless-filled evening and it was 'bath night'. The tin bath would be placed in front of the fire and after my brother had been bathed it would be my turn. What luxury. We only had a bath once a week, so it was something to look forward to; especially so because at the same time the wireless was switched on straight after the football results (which my father and grandfather did jointly but never won) and the news, and we listened to *Dick Barton, Special Agent*, followed by *Lost in Space*. The signature tune of the former was very memorable and many people of my age can still hum it.

Dick Barton was one of the first super-sleuths (after Conan Doyle's Sherlock Holmes, of course). He was assisted in a (by now) well-tried formula, by his not-so-bright assistants Jock and Snowy. The series started in around 1946 and lasted until 1951. Wonderful stuff! *Lost in Space* also became a thrilling series, but not one after which to go to bed if you were of a nervous disposition. The BBC Radiophonics Workshop had not yet been created but the BBC technicians went to town on the weird and scary sound effects the series called for.

Whilst touching on scary things, I must mention how scared we were when we were cut off for several days during the harsh winter of 1951.

It followed on the heels of the terrible winter of 1947, when the country was in the grip of a national emergency. The government had to call in troops to try and keep even the railways clear and there was a serious possibility of widespread starvation. They had to harvest root crops with pneumatic drills and few ships were able to move because the ports were frozen over too (the Taff and the Cardiff canals also froze). Many people died of the cold or starvation and it happened just as the Americans cut off further aid for us.

Our house was one of many where the kitchen was a peninsular extending into the yard. I remember vividly that the entire void between our house and next door was completely filled with snow. The glass conservatory had been covered completely and one of its panes had broken letting in snow which piled up on the cooker and sink. As a result of the danger presented by the breaking of further panes of glass, my grandparents had to live in the same room as us.

Although this helped us to conserve heat, so much snow had fallen that it was impossible to open the back door (which opened outwards) to go outside to the toilet or to collect coal for the fire. The window in the living room was totally covered by snow to a depth of around 9 feet, the resulting pressure threatening to burst it. We therefore had to keep well away from the window and stayed largely in the front room where a roaring fire was lit. But how long could the fire last?

It was decided that my father and grandfather, together with a few neighbours, would dig their way from the front of the house, where the snow had not blocked the door because it was sheltered by the porch, to the back of the house – a long way. They decided to dig along the pavement and down the lane, so as to be able to free the toilets and coal houses. What adventure! Would they make it? Would they ever return? Looking from my parents' upstairs bedroom windows the men could be seen throwing the snow high in the air, creating even higher walls of snow over the already several feet or so of snow.

Snow drift

In the house, as our supply of coal dwindled, we fell back on a form of heating much used by everyone: the paraffin stove. Bearing in mind that central heating was not to be seen for many years yet, only one room at a time was heated and the bedrooms never, unless someone was ill in bed.

The paraffin heater helped to take the chill off rooms and melt the ice on the windows. It was a very old, black device that stood about 2 feet 6 inches tall. It is shown in the photograph.

It had a reservoir for the oil in the base, which was fairly wide and round like the rest of it. Made of steel, it was covered in decorative cut-outs, notably in the top, which had a slide on it whereby more or fewer of the holes in it could be opened up or closed down. Warm air from the flame of the wick rose through it and exited mainly through the top, casting beautiful patterns on the ceiling if it was dark. The stove was finished in shiny black enamel.

We bought the paraffin at a shop on Corporation Road - Davey's. Mr Davey was, I think, a bachelor and his mother lived with him. The shop was very bare; it had linoleum on the floor and smelled strongly of paraffin, which he kept in two large oil drums turned on their sides and supported in wooden saddles. Each was equipped with a tap and both were in the front of the shop. He also sold oil, turpentine, varnish and similar liquids. So the shop had a nice smell.

He would measure out the paraffin into a steel measuring jug with a long spout on it and filled whatever storage device the customer had brought. All pretty dangerous I suppose, especially if a customer came in smoking. The only other items on sale seemed to be Blackfriars paint, of which he had a comprehensive stock. Thankfully, we had bought a fresh supply of paraffin from Davey's as the weather worsened, so we were reasonably well prepared.

Paraffin heater

It took a day for the men to reach the back of the houses by digging a channel. For me, a child, it was an amazing scene. The channel was barely wide enough for an adult, but to me it was a canyon, whose walls towered above me. Such an emergency changed our priorities completely. For example, we didn't know what was happening about school, except we couldn't get there. Subsequently, we discovered that the school had to be shut for a week in order to repair the damage caused by frozen pipes and a burst boiler.

The wartime habit of hoarding food and essential supplies meant that not having access to the shops for a while wasn't too much of a problem, except for obtaining fresh food such as bread and milk. My mother always held a large stock of tinned food beneath her bed in two old suitcases. She continued this habit well into her old age. Any imaginable tinned food was available under the bed and in fair quantities.

The main problem caused by the snow was getting fuel from the coal house outside and stopping the water pipes from freezing. Unfortunately, the pipes in the outside loo had frozen solid by the time Dad reached it, but my grandfather managed to thaw much of it with his paraffin-powered blow-lamp. He had to be especially careful doing this, because the piping was of lead, which melts at quite a low temperature.

At least we still had a gas supply and intermittent electricity. We could listen to the wireless and get the latest national news, but could get no local news of Cardiff. We weren't getting newspapers and we had no telephone, so getting local news was impossible. For this we relied on word of mouth and the police when the roads were clear enough. In such weather lots of things were damaged: car radiators burst when they thawed out; tram lines twisted and broke; a number of horses died in the fields, as did large numbers of cattle. The steel works and gasworks sheltered many a person caught out in the snow, unable to get home and unable to communicate with their families.

Perhaps that was the worst effect of the storm: our communications broke down. The telephone system relied on individual wires attached to china insulators on top of telegraph poles (underground cables weren't used until the 60s): they were thus fully exposed to the storm. They consisted of quite soft copper wire that shrank considerably in low temperatures and snapped easily under the weight of ice and the force of the wind. The china insulators were very fragile too and many broke under the tension of the wires, sometimes even pulling the wooden poles over as they too snapped or bent.

**

To grown-ups, this winter weather was a serious worry. To us children, it was great fun and very memorable, much of the fun made possible by having wellingtons to wear – pity the child who didn't have any. Which prompts me to describe what I always thought as an amusing item of footwear: galoshes.

This invention takes its name from the French *galoche* or working overshoe. They were made of soft rubber and worn so as to entirely cover a shoe. Once at work or school, the galosh was lifted off the shoe and hey presto you had dry shiny shoes.

They were strange things, because although they were made of fairly thin rubber (otherwise it would be difficult to slide them over shoes) the result was to have feet that appeared huge. Many men wore them when it rained, especially when going to church, say, or in my grandfather's case to a meeting of his lodge, The Royal and Ancient Order of Foresters. These were formal meetings and he needed to turn up with presentable shoes; or ankle-length boots in his case because I never saw him wear shoes.

When hearing that he belonged to the Foresters, I assumed he was a member of some especially honoured citizens who were given the right to walk down the middle of the high street dressed in Sherwood green, armed with a bow and a full quiver full of arrows. But it was not to be: it was just a friendly society for saving and borrowing money. I was so disappointed.

Bearing in mind people either walked everywhere (whatever the weather) or got a bus, keeping leather shoes dry when it rained was an important issue. Also, anyone not having clean, polished shoes was thought of as lazy and slovenly. These were taken as indicators of moral integrity rated highly alongside having trousers that were well pressed. So keeping shoes polished, dry and clean was important to one's sense of decency.

For men, these sartorial habits were the equivalent of housewives keeping the doorstep of the house clean and even washing the pavement outside; stone steps or thresholds being cleaned by scrubbing with a soft stone, added to the twice-weekly use of *Brasso* on the brass letterbox and door knocker. These were favourite bob-a-job tasks for cubs, scouts and guides.

The pavements in front of houses were also kept clear of moss and weeds. One of my much-liked tasks was to be given an old kitchen knife and asked to scrape the moss and dirt from between the paving stones outside the house, even in the gutter. Most houses had this clean and proud look about them, even in the darkest corners of Grangetown and the docks.

* * *

Which brings me finally to something a little naughty for which knockers and letterboxes were intended, or so we children thought. The story also illustrates that we weren't all saints!

It was the game of 'Rat-Tat-Ginger', the origin of the name being a mystery to me, especially the use of 'ginger', which is odd. It was a simple game played only on streets where neighbours' doors were directly adjacent to each other and without porches.

The trick was to connect a piece of string to the door knocker of one house, pull it so that it wasn't too loose and tie the other end to the door knocker of the adjacent house. Then, lift the knocker of one house and run as fast as you could and hide, but in such a place that allows you to see the result. The person answering the door pulls the string as he or she tries to open their door, thus knocking the knocker of the other house, the occupant of which then tries to open *their* door, and so on! It was naughty really, and we reserved the game for use on people who had been generally nasty to us, such

The never-ending task of washing the steps

as those who never returned footballs that we accidentally kicked over their walls.

The end point of this cowardly game was to watch the neighbours negotiate through cracks in their front doors, usually shouting to be heard and deciding which of them should get out of their house via the back lane and walk around the block to the front door to detach the string preventing the doors from opening.

It's amazing what fun can be had with just a little string - and of course that old lump of chalk.

Lightning Source UK Ltd.
Milton Keynes UK
UKHW030743310822
408116UK00006B/612